GUIDED IMAGERY AND MUSIC
IN THE INSTITUTIONAL SETTING

Lisa Summer, RMT-BC

MMB MUSIC, INC.

MMB Horizon Series

THE LOTUS FLOWER

Held sacred by the ancients in the Near and Far East, the lotus flower has an uninterrupted symbolic history of over 5,000 years. It is a symbol for hope, faith and renewed life as it closes its petals at night, sinking beneath the water, only to rise and open again with the sunrise.

This flower was chosen to represent this series as a symbol of our hope and faith in therapy, special education, rehabilitation medicine, the helping professions and in the development of individuals to their fullest potential.

GUIDED IMAGERY AND MUSIC
IN THE INSTITUTIONAL SETTING

Lisa Summer, RMT-BC

ISBN 0-918812-57-7
PRINTED IN USA

Cover Artwork: Eunice Summer
Typography: Gary K. Lee
Third Printing: September 1997
Printer: John S. Swift Company, Inc., Saint Louis, MO

For further information and catalogs, contact:

MMB Music, Inc.
Contempoary Arts Building
3526 Washington Avenue
Saint Louis, MO 63103-1019 USA

Phone: 314 531-9635, 800 543-3771 (USA/Canada)
Fax: 314 531-8384
E-mail: mmbmusic@mmbmusic.com
Web site: http://www.mmbmusic.com

This book is dedicated to Joe, my husband.

CONTENTS

ABOUT THE AUTHOR

After honing her craft as a French hornist, Lisa Summer entered the field of music therapy, acquiring her degrees at Western Michigan University and Hahnemann University. She began her clinical work while concurrently studying with Helen Bonny at the Institute for Consciousness and Music in the specialized field of GIM. Continuing a private practice in GIM, and incorporating her expertise in GIM into her music therapy work in institutional settings, Lisa became convinced of the importance of GIM as a tool in music therapy clinical work. She has pioneered an adapted form of GIM for use with groups from which experience this book grew.

Lisa is Coordinator of GIM Programs at the Bonny Foundation for Music-Centered Therapies, overseeing a three-year postgraduate GIM program which trains future GIM practitioners in dyad and group GIM. She and Helen Bonny, in tandem, lead several one- and two-week training workshops every year and are currently collaborating on the Foundation's Advanced GIM training program.

Currently Lisa is Associate Professor/Director of Music Therapy at Anna Maria College near Boston, MA. She is editor of the *Music Therapy International Report* and author of the book *Music: The New Age Elixir*, a critical survey of music healers. Lisa continues to promote active musicianship as an important element in every music therapist's life through both the AMC program and the Bonny Foundation training. She lives (and plays music) with her opera composer husband, Joseph, and her 13-year-old daughter, Eve, a self-proclaimed ballerina.

FOREWORD

Helen Bonny

Those of us who have chosen music therapy as a career face a dilemma. In our love and appreciation of music we intuitively acknowledge its power, yet as professionals in the healing arts we also recognize the need to justify the use of music as a therapy. We are torn between the demands for an exact science proclaimed by the current helping professions (which ascribe value based on the prevailing availability of a financial base) and our firm belief that music is and can be that medium most adept at providing healing to the client irrespective of a scientifically based procedure. To satisfy one is often to do damage to the other. There are several reasons why music therapy must dance the razor's edge in order to meet its goals. They may be listed as (1) the difference in the range of action of the medium, (2) the ideology which the musician and the nonmusician carries into their work, and (3) the goals and expectations regarding the belief system under which the therapist is operating.

The Action of the Medium

Therapists other than those of the arts use a verbal action or its equivalent as the primary mode of expression. The speaking voice, our common way of communicating our emotions and needs, has a range of action that is limited to what we call a linear or line effect. Our utterances, made in a normal state of conscious attention, communicate information of a practical or social nature. Only when the voice is used in a musical way, as with song, does the linear, or line representation change to the multidimensional mode.

Music, on the other hand, because of its inherent nature, is intrinsically many-leveled and therefore more complex in its action. The physical components of each tone, which in most instruments comprise an arrangement of harmonic frequencies of different and varying energies, are within themselves analyzed by the listener for far more elements (pitch, relation to other pitches, duration, and timbre) than speech. Add several notes together—as we are accustomed to hearing them in musical pieces from piano sonatas to Mahler's *Symphony of a Thousand*—and a person's linear level of conscious attention is diverted into a computerlike diversity of signals which must reach into myriad levels of our essence. Given this action of the medium of music we find ourselves in an unfamiliar venue and must ask, "How can music which creates such diverse and endless interactions in the human body, be squeezed into the codification of traditional linear research models?"

The question can be posed as an illustration: Think of placing a verbal comment on an imaginary spectrogram. You can reproduce one easily by taking a paper and pencil, and, as you ask a question, allow the poised pencil to raise and lower in a continuous line across the page to represent the higher and lower frequencies of the voice. Now do the same thing with a short musical selection. You will soon find that one pencil is not enough. You need to use at least as many pencils as there are individual instruments merely to capture the fundamental frequencies. To analyze the addition and subtraction frequencies and timbres you would need an army of scribes. (It would be much simpler to purchase the score.)

We then translate this experience into a therapeutic setting where frequency of voice versus musical range is compounded by other variables such as loudness, pitch, dynamic expression, emotional quality, ease of modes of communication, and you can surmise the differences in the two mediums. Further, you can appreciate the greatly extended range for potential information retrieval the musical range may supply. Music therapists are just beginning to appreciate the full and extended possibilities which are inherent in their medium. In this book Lisa Summer is grappling with the seemingly endless possibilities which Guided Imagery and Music presents to the therapists, and she is finding that the range is often too wide to safely confine her work with specific clients. The reader will be wise to heed her comments in Chapter 10, "The Use of GIM with Various Populations."

Ideology of Musician Versus Nonmusician

There is always a danger in assigning beliefs to a group or category of persons, especially if the determining factor is related to their principal profession. To say that musicians are "this" or "that" as opposed to nonmusicians is a simplification of a complex situation in which a host of variables must be scrutinized. But it must be acknowledged that the making of a musician demands qualities within the person and a life-view that is not often shared by the nonmusician. What are these differences? To know them may help us understand the ideology behind our profession.

First, let us look at the many hours of practice demanded of the performer to perfect the craft. Isolated from social interaction, highly concentrated in moment by moment attention to the subtleties of tone, technique, dynamics, and interpretation, the performer becomes involved in a world of symbolic interaction which does not reflect the politics of the conscious everyday world. As the performer is practicing his instrument he is at the same time practicing the art of opening doors on many levels of his person to the music medium. This refers not alone to music but to all types of symbolic experience. The pump is being primed for the aesthetic to occur. This deep satisfaction creates a desire in the musician, who in addition is drawn to the healing mode, to reproduce this rich and rewarding experience for the client. On a personal level the music therapist is deeply aware that the aesthetic quality of the musical experience has been healing and revitalizing for them and they wish therefore to reproduce the experience for others. We can say that the ideology of wishing to be helpful is similar for musician and nonmusician. The differences occur in the mode, quality, and depth of response which is made possible through using music as the "voice."

Goals and Expectations

Clinical practice in the United States is dictated by a terminology based on psychiatry and psychology and is espoused by practitioners who are devoted to specific theoretical bases. Through the tempering actions of research and practice these bases are translated into an established theory which eventually becomes quite widespread and accepted. The limitations of such widespread acceptance lie in a descriptive terminology that becomes solidified in meaning and limits language use.

An example of solidified meaning is found in the term "paranoia," an abnormal tendency to suspect and mistrust others. Originally it was used exclusively as a description of a mental disorder involving delusions of persecution or grandeur. Today pop psychology has generalized usage to mean any fearful reaction not easily understood by the observer. It becomes a term that codifies and limits all possible experience which relates to fear reactions. As a therapist I find that my work with clients using music and imagery is of such depth as to bypass such codifications. Fear can arise from a complex series of justifications and symbolically reveal itself in numerous ways, many of which are reasonable and normal.

How then will the music therapist, with a greater range of therapeutic material in which to work, encompass the procedure and define the work? One of the many ways being discovered is Guided Imagery and Music (GIM). Relatively new as a therapeutic practice, the GIM procedure has an ancient precedence in the Aesculapian cults of the Greeks. More recently, as states of consciousness have been defined, music, too, has found its place as a catalyst. Jungian theory has achieved scientific respectability; the creative imagination, the collective unconscious, and the archetypal dream have become considerations for everyday practice. With these have come new appreciation for the arts. The potential for arts therapies is great and can benefit from a careful formulation of theory and practice to match present enthusiasms. In this book you will find a beginning and a positive new direction for music therapy clinical practice.

Lisa Summer: A Personal Note

An annual music therapy conference is a big event. Anxiety reigns as expectation of greeting old and new faces and discussing shared problems mix with the reality of exposing your year's work to colleagues. Exposing your work is the hardest. It becomes a delight when student energy is released in bursts of interest, enthusiasm, and even skepticism. Eager faces lift for crumbs of insights (and they are crumbs) as colleagues ask probing questions (and on occasion turn a deaf ear to your meticulously earned findings).

1976 was a good year. Many students pressing into the conference room made a move to a larger room necessary, asking questions, wanting to learn more; and one of them was Lisa with dark, intense eyes which did not release mine until she was satisfied, and that meant my agreeing that she come to Baltimore to train in GIM at the Institute for Consciousness and Music.

In her two years of training Lisa never swerved from her first enthusiasms, although it meant long and tiresome work at mundane jobs to cover her expenses. The GIM training is tutorial. Long hours are spent in learning the practice from your own personal interior work, in imagery, in music; and later in the program you are supervised as you give sessions to others. Attendance at numerous workshops, as an assistant in the phase training, writing reports and case histories, helping to teach others; all these were involved in Lisa's program.

Never far away was our mutual love of and joy in making music together. How many times did we pull out the Brahms Horn Trio, or sight read some new composition which Lisa's composer-husband Joe had found for us?

Active involvement in playing music was the perfect balance for the intense passive listening that GIM practice demanded and it deepened our primary contact with the "mother voice." As Lisa will say in this book, the GIM facilitator and the music become as one in the experience of the traveler-client. The blurring of boundaries as experienced by the client can motivate a less personally oriented transference and glue its easing magic onto a musical composition, to be channeled and ingrained in the psyche at fundamental levels. It seems imperative, therefore, in the training of facilitators, to involve their music-making skills to reveal insight and to provide/allow for personal balance.

Sensitivity to human needs is the mark of a fine music therapist. In the final paragraphs of "Guided Imagery and Music with the Elderly" (1981) Summer amplifies the quality of her ideological approach to clients and discloses the warmth and concern which preside over her practice:

> Each person's individuality, no matter how distasteful or unacceptable to the professional, should be taken into account in therapy. If aspects of the psyche are silenced, the result can be an unsatisfactory life. On the other hand, if we recognize and work with these integral parts of the personality, then we are encouraging a meaningful life for the individual.

INTRODUCTION

In music we begin to live eternally in the present and are given the infinity of true musical space. —from *The Psychoanalysis of Artistic Vision and Hearing* by Anton Ehrenzweig

Regardless of which source one uses, there is universal accord that Aesculapius, the world's first doctor, learned his art at the feet of Apollo, god of music.[1] As music therapists we witness daily the relationship between music and healing, and should not refrain from singing praise to music in its capacity as a facilitator to health. One powerful technique, Guided Imagery and Music (GIM), has not previously been readily available to the music therapist due to reasons which do not reflect on its wide applicability to our clients. The primary motivation for me in writing *Guided Imagery and Music in the Institutional Setting* is to help music therapists discover the benefits of GIM and to encourage the dissemination of information needed for GIM to take its rightful place in the repertoire of music therapy techniques.

GIM is a technique in which the act of listening to classical music is combined with a relaxed state of mind and body in order to evoke imagery for the purpose of self-actualization. The imagery evoked reflects aspects of the self and is used by the client, with the aid of the GIM-trained music therapist, to effectuate positive growth towards the aforementioned purpose. The ultimate goal of GIM, in accordance with the basic tenets of humanistic therapy, is the transcendence of the individual ego.

Previously GIM has required an expensive and lengthy commitment. My own training took place in Baltimore with Marilyn Clark and Helen Bonny, GIM's founder. At ICM I learned how to use GIM in a one-to-one setting in private practice. With Helen Bonny's guidance I undertook the task of using GIM in institutional settings, first in several Baltimore area nursing homes, and later (after earning my "Fellow" degree through my work with the elderly) in a private psychiatric hospital, a special school, and a community music school in Philadelphia where I worked with both adults and children of normal and special populations. Some of my work with the various groups is noted in this book.

Any music therapist with an intense commitment is the perfect candidate for GIM training. Candidates need to be mature adults, with a graduate degree. Training in GIM includes experiencing GIM as a client in order to learn the language of imagery and mastery of the technique; supervision of group and individual GIM sessions; and a study of the specifics of the technique (how to conduct a prelude and postlude, stimulate altered states of consciousness through relaxation and induction techniques, choose music to facilitate the music/imagery synergy, guide, and work toward therapeutic goals). In addition the candidate needs to have a knowledge of the population(s) with which he intends to practice the technique.

The practice of GIM requires tutelage with a trained GIM practitioner. This book is not intended (nor can it be used) as a substitute for this tutelage, but rather should serve as a theoretical study for clinicians, students, and educators, as well as an adjunctive text for GIM practitioners interested in applying the technique in institutional and group settings. I can appreciate the desire to use GIM. It is an exciting therapeutic tool. But GIM is not without its hazards, and the contraindications for its use, detailed in Chapter 10, do not begin to cover the dynamic potential of a GIM session, even when used with normal clients. For the clinician, student, or educator who wishes to apply aspects of GIM in their work I have outlined several GIM-related activities in Chapter 9.

---

[1]Indeed, most sources report the mythical Aesculapius as being Apollo's son.

Training for clinical work in GIM is available at the Bonny Foundation for Music-Centered Therapies in Salina, Kansas. The Association for Music and Imagery (AMI) has been formed to disseminate information about GIM through journals and conferences and AMI-approved GIM training programs are available through institutes and universities in the United States, Canada, and in Europe. I will hazard being redundant by commenting that it is my fervent wish that this book will encourage the growth of the use of GIM by music therapists in clinical practice and inaugurate training in the use of GIM in institutional settings.

ACKNOWLEDGMENTS

This book could not have been written without the 1986 and 1987 Phoenicia community: the providence and continual guidance of Helen Bonny, the astute advice of Barbara Hesser, the support of Rachel Verney, Sara Jane Stokes, Lisa Sokolov, Even Ruud, Clive Robbins, Carol Robbins, Carolyn Kenny, David Gonzalez, Joanne Crandall, and David Burrows.

I take this opportunity to thank Sharon Pirrone at MMB for her support, and the clients from Northwestern Institute for Psychiatry whose imagery permeates this book.

ONE

IMAGERY

Bottom: (Awakening) When my cue comes, call me, and I will answer: my next is, "most fair Pyramus." Heigh-ho! Peter Quince! Flute the bellows-mender! Snout, the tinker! Starveling! God's my life, stolen hence, and left me asleep! I have had a dream, past the wit of man to say what dream it was: man is but an ass, if he go about to expound this dream. Methought I was—there is no man can tell what. Methought I was,—and methought I had,—but man is but a patched fool, if he will offer to say what methought I had. The eye of man hath not heard, the ear of man hath not seen, man's hand is not able to taste, his tongue to conceive, nor his heart to report, what my dream was. I will get Peter Quince to write a ballad of this dream: it shall be called Bottom's Dream, because it hath no bottom; and I will sing it in the latter end of a play, before the duke: peradventure, to make it the more gracious I shall sing it at her death.
—from *A Midsummer Night's Dream* by Shakespeare

We are what we imagine. Though the external world may exist as an objective reality, no one will ever be able to prove it. In physics, mathematics, and psychology we are faced with the insoluble dilemma of the effect of the observer upon the observed. The anxiety the philosopher feels when confronting the dichotomy between subjective and objective reality may be no different than that of the infant driven by hunger to create fulfillment, a fulfillment that belongs to his inner world. An imagined breast, though objectively unreal, is experienced as real in all senses. The infant sees, smells, feels, tastes and experiences the full gamut of emotions, including satisfaction, just as he would during an objectively real feeding. The child learns not only to recreate what is absent, but also to retain the feelings associated with it. Thus, the image, the phantasm of the inner world, substitutes for external reality. "Images," says Arieti, "soon constitute the basic level of the inner psychic reality which in psychology is as important as, and in some respects more important than, external reality." As the child matures, the use of imagery becomes less self-deluding and more sophisticated.

Arieti's definition of imagery, "An internal quasi-reproduction of a perception that does not require the corresponding external stimulus in order to be evoked" (Arieti 1967, 63), is useful for understanding the basic concept of imagery. It serves however, as no more than a starting point for theorists who have found this definition inadequate to express the importance of imagery in human behavior.

Obvious to anyone who has had a dream, our inner world does not consist solely of visual elements. Who has not, during a nightmare, found himself running "as if through water?" This common form of imagery is labeled "kinaesthetic" by Sheehan based upon work by Betts. Along with visual and kinaesthetic modes, Sheehan catalogs auditory (such as the sound of escaping steam), cutaneous (the sensation of a pin prick), gustatory (the taste of an orange), olfactory (the smell of cooking cabbage), and organic (the sensation of drowsiness) (Sheehan 1967).

Sarbin, wearying of the more prosaic attempts at defining imagery, stresses the nature of involvement in imagining. He believes "pictures in the mind" and "imaging as a passive process" produce virtually nothing pragmatically useful. The prevalent attitude of accepting passive reception of "impressions and ideas flitting hither and yon in mental space according to the laws of association" as the epitome of the use of imagery in therapy has contributed to an attitude wherein "most thinkers have regarded imagining as something akin to a tendency for bibulousness or tippling: it is tolerated, even approved of in moderation but too much of it is to be frowned on, it leads to monkish, bohemian, artistic, and other forms of supposedly disreputable behavior." He proposes changing the passive acceptance of fanciful imaginings into a dynamic tool for psychological problem solving. After all, man is not simply a receptacle into which surrealistic ideas float unprompted, but is an active manipulator, exploring and changing his external and internal environment. The action of imagining an alteration in his environment is the quintessential element differentiating man from beast; his ability to hypothesize. Before he acts, he can imagine the consequences of his proposed action. He can create an "as if" world. In therapy the "as if" world is a powerful tool available to the therapist in dealing with internal thoughts and feelings and their relation to external reality. The mere imagining of a situation causes authentic physiological and emotional reactions "as if" it were actually occurring (Sarbin and Juhasz 1970, 62).

Categories of Imagery

In his task of categorizing the various definitions of imagery, Horowitz (1970) provides one of the best overviews of the subject. His categories are vividness, content, context, and interaction with perception.

The first category, vividness, includes hallucinations, pseudohallucinations, thought images, and unconscious images contrasted by their degree of vividness, that is, their apparent reality. Unconscious images are deemed fairly vivid, hallucinations are the most vivid. A hallucination is by definition nearly impossible to differentiate from reality. Insights, such as those that might be characterized by a physicist as quantum leaps (without a logical rhetorical sequence) need to be added to Horowitz's first category. The "aha!" phenomenon, a very vivid variant of the thought image, is experienced often in therapeutic settings (especially regarding transference), altered states of consciousness, and of course, in creative problem solving.

Images categorized by content constitute memory images (a reconstruction of a past perception), imaginary images, entoptic images (physiologically induced visual images caused by stimulation of optic structures of the eye or in optic neural circuits), and sundry minor visual phenomena. In order to make Horowitz's second category more accurate and comprehensive it is necessary to incorporate the work of Sheehan. The newly augmented category would include kinaesthetic, auditory, gustatory, cutaneous (tactile), organic, and olfactory imagery.

The circumstances under which imagery occurs define the category Horowitz labels "context." This category contains dream images, psychedelic images (drug induced), hypnagogic or hypnopompic images (sleep related), flashbacks (unbidden return of images formed during drug intoxication), and dream scintillations (flickering images while conscious). A serious lacuna in this category is music-induced imagery, which must be considered separate from hypnagogic because by definition hypnagogic imagery can be produced only in the state between wakefulness and sleep. Nevertheless both music-induced and hypnagogic imagery are remarkably similar. Both differ from other forms of imagery in the clarity of their form and content, which permits exact description. In addition, imagery produced by either of the two has a distinct life of its own, although never beyond conscious control. Leuner maintains that hypnagogic imagery "contain(s) meaningful symbols analogous to the symbols of dreams. They differ from those in dreams in their comparative simplicity and clarity of content. Most important, relevant psychodynamic organization is projected into such (imagery) far more clearly than is found in dreams" (Leuner 1965).

Imagery is affected by the external (objective) world. Regardless of how inwardly focused the imager is, external stimuli will affect the experience to some degree. Returning to Arieti's definition of the image as not requiring external stimulus, Horowitz and others maintain that, whereas no external stimulus is required nevertheless it is there; and its presence has an effect upon imagery. The interaction of image content with an outwardly perceived object: a percept, (Horowitz's fourth category) may be observed in deja vu experiences (the illusion of familiarity), negative hallucinations (not seeing something that is there), perceptual distortion, afterimages, and synaesthesia. All the modes of imagery experienced during GIM are affected by the external stimulus, the music. The imagery produced during GIM may be invariably considered to fall into Horowitz's third and fourth categories and in specific details, may concurrently fall into the first or second categories.

TWO

THE USE OF MUSIC TO STIMULATE IMAGERY

Peter:	*Musicians, O, musicians, "Heart's ease, Heart's ease:" O, an you will have me live, play "heart's ease."*
1st musician:	*Why "heart's ease"?*
Peter:	*O, musicians, because my heart itself plays "my heart is full of woe:" O, play me some merry dump, to comfort me.*
1st musician:	*Not a dump we; 'tis no time to play now.*
Peter:	*You will not then?*
1st musician:	*No.*
Peter:	*I will then give it you soundly... I will carry no crotchets: I'll re you, I'll fa you; do you note me?*
1st musician:	*An you re us and fa us, you note us.*
2nd musician:	*Pray you, put up your dagger, and put out your wit.*
Peter:	*Then have at you with my wit! I will dry-beat you with an iron with, and put up my iron dagger. Answer me like men:* *"WHEN GRIPING GRIEF THE HEART DOTH WOUND, AND DOLEFUL DUMPS THE MIND OPPRESS, THEN MUSIC WITH HER SILVER SOUND—"* *Why "silver sound?" Why "music with her silver sound?" What say you, Simon Catling? ...I will say for you. It is "music with her silver sound," because musicians have no gold for sounding:* *"THEN MUSIC WITH HER SILVER SOUND WITH SPEEDY HELP DOTH LEND REDRESS."*

—from *Romeo and Juliet* by Shakespeare

Often therapists make the mistaken assumption that what is popular is good. Certainly recognizing what is popular is essential to our well being and our daily intercourse with society. Nevertheless, we should not confuse the concept of popularity with significance. GIM calls for both the therapist and the client to explore the most significant aspects of their psyche. Trivial music would certainly be a hindrance and possibly a barrier to self-actualization.

Classical music (by classical music I mean art music of the western culture, not restricted to the more specific Classical period) is the only music that can be used for GIM. It is multileveled, stimulating, and connects inner experiences. Often it stimulates archetypal imagery, a peak experience linked to inner spiritual and existential issues. Classical music has no fixed meaning, thus the imagery it stimulates has no boundary in its contents. Classical music expands the aesthetic horizons of its listeners, opening them to a fuller appreciation of their environment. "A masterwork," said Aaron Copland, "awakens in us reactions of a spiritual order that are already in us, only waiting to be aroused" (Copland 1952, 17).

A piece of popular music most often arouses our mental image of the performer or performers. Interestingly, this very facet of popular music extends to the more recent genre of music videos in which, with rare exception, the performing artist is the central image in the video. Not only does popular music stimulate rigidly defined visual images, but also does the same in regard to its text. Nearly all popular music is vocal. The specific messages have shallow, fixed meanings, and ask us to react to the performer's specific personal dilemma.

In GIM the therapist guides the client through a melange of imagery and experiences. Because of the simplistic structure of popular music, it does not evoke a fluid, moving imagery, but rather a stasis congruent with its repetitiousness.

For those elements just mentioned popular music works well in music therapy techniques where clients need a specific agenda and where inward movement is threatening. There is no doubt that popular music may evoke a vigorous physical response which is highly desirable in specific instances. Note that the physical response to popular music is another detracting element in relation to GIM, where the least amount of physical motion is preferred.

In GIM the body is relaxed so that the mind may be active and undistracted by the external environment. But the physical state of the client is a means to an end, and not the end in itself. GIM is not relaxation and music which is designed to create solely a state of relaxation is not of use in GIM. Currently it is popular to use "new age" music for relaxation. This also includes minimalist music and environmental sound collages. This music is characterized by unabashed repetitiousness, a relative lack of dissonance, and extremely simplistic structure. "New age" music is a spiritual descendant of the religious music of the Orient which is used as an adjunct to meditation.

In order to establish a link between client and therapist, the therapist might be tempted to employ in the GIM session music which is the client's stated preference. Though preferences should be noted for other techniques and as diagnostic information, the use of client preferred music in GIM creates problems similar to those found with the use of popular music, that is, specific and rigid associations that draw the client out of an altered state and into an alert state of consciousness associated with his listening habits. Tangentially significant may be Rider's study of pain reduction and imagery where he notes that "client preferred" music is not as effective in reducing pain as other prescribed types (Rider 1985).

"Classical music," wrote Helen Bonny in *Music Therapy: A Legal High*, "was more useful than the popular categories as it…provided an emotional frame of reference. Pop, rock and jazz, for the most part, directed the listener's attention to itself rather than an aid or vehicle for personal experience. (Classical) Music can be used again and again without getting 'stale' " (Bonny and Tansill 1977, 122).

THE HISTORY OF GIM

Pliny says that there is a certain land in which neither dew nor rain falls. Consequently, there is a general aridness; but in this country there is a single fountain, from which, when people would draw water, they are accustomed to approach with all kinds of musical instruments, and so march around it for a length of time. The melody which they thus produce causes the water to rise to the mouth of the spring, and makes it flow forth in great abundance, so that all men are able to obtain as much as they will. —from the *Gesta Romanorum*

Both Freud and Jung used imagery with their patients in exploring the unconscious. Freud used hypnosis and Jung used an active imagination technique, but Leuner (1969) was the first psychiatrist to develop a formal method for using imagery in therapy. Colored by his own views of what was important to a patient's mental betterment, Leuner developed a method of intensive psychotherapy that stressed subconscious motivation, the significance of symbols, and resistance. Through the mobilization of affect, Leuner sought to relieve acute neurotic disturbances, neuroses, and psychosomatic and borderline conditions.

In the manner of his predecessors, Leuner would have his patient lie down on a couch; but in a departure from tradition the patient would first participate in a short relaxation technique. Then Leuner would utilize one of his ten imagery inductions to begin the therapy. Depending upon the patient's specific problems, Leuner would have him imagine either (1) a meadow, (2) a mountain, (3) a brook, (4) a house, (5) a relative, (6) a rosebush, or other sexual symbol, (7) a lion, (8) an ego ideal, such as Moses, (9) a phantasmagorical creature, or (10) an archetypal figure. The therapy consisted of Leuner manipulating the imagery of the patient that had been evoked during the induction. Thus, if the seventh induction had been used and the patient had expressed fear of the lion, Leuner might suggest that he feed and befriend it. Following the imagery session Leuner would analyze the patient's experience based on Leuner's own restricted view of the meaning of his symbolic inductions. Thus, because in Leuner's symbolic lexicon lions mean anger, he would interpret the patient's reactions in the imagery as representative of those that he has in his life regarding his anger. Each image as symbol had a concomitant definition in real life. Though flawed by his overly specific interpretations, Leuner's technique could, and did work, because the act of working on problems in an altered state of consciousness (such as that induced by Leuner) enhances emotions, generates quantum leaps in problem solving, and (through confrontation with the problem) results in a strengthening of the ego.

What Leuner had in common with his predecessors Freud and Jung, was a desire to reach into the subconscious; the only path to which lay through imagery. Leuner's method for invoking imagery was a step forward in the field. However, neither his, nor Freud's, nor Jung's approaches could guarantee the near 100 percent success of altering the brain's consciousness through physical manipulation of the organ of thought itself. Once scientists had developed the tools for entry into the brain it was inevitable that therapeutic fields would adopt them.

Specific chemicals developed to ameliorate specific neurochemical problems are the standard treatment of many mental illnesses. Amidst the development of these "Brave New World" chemical agents, LSD was synthesized. In the 1960s two hospitals, the Maryland Psychiatric Research Center (MPRC) and the Veterans Administration Hospital in Topeka began to experiment with the use of LSD and music in the treatment of terminally ill patients and substance abusers. Working with the Topeka group, Gaston and Eagle reported that though LSD could induce mental distortions resembling psychosis, it could also help people face painful realities of disease and death, and point out solutions to problems with interpersonal relationships (Gaston and Eagle 1970). In Maryland, psychiatrists reported that after a peak experience during LSD therapy, "Mood is elevated and energetic; there is a relative freedom from concerns of the past and from guilt and anxiety, and the disposition and capacity to enter into close interpersonal relationships is enhanced. These psychedelic feelings generally persist for two weeks to a month and then gradually fade into vivid memories that hopefully will still influence attitude and behavior. During this immediate postdrug period, there is a unique opportunity for effective psychotherapeutic work on strained family or other interpersonal relationships" (Pahnke et al. 1970, p. 1858). In Maryland, experimental patients ingesting LSD experienced a 10- to 12-hour period of intense drug-altered consciousness. Prerecorded music was played, chosen by Helen Bonny according to the intensity of the drug experience. In her article, "The Use of Music in Psychedelic (LSD) Therapy" Bonny describes a typical guided "trip" as consisting of six periods:

1. Preonset (0 to 1.5 hours) during which a light popular or patient-preferred selection is played.
2. Onset (0.5 to 1.5 hours) during which the LSD begins to have a definite impact, quiet, reassuring music is played.
3. Building toward peak (1.5 to 3 hours) during which music with insistent rhythms and long phrases is played.
4. Peak intensity (3 to 4.5 hours) during which powerful music with strong structure is played.
5. Reentry (4.5 to 7 hours) during which quiet, peaceful music is played.
6. Return to normal consciousness (7 to 12 hours) during which music from the session is replayed (Bonny and Pahnke 1972).

As a result of LSD/music therapy with 117 alcoholics, it was found that the group of patients who had "experienced the most profound psychedelic peak experience had the highest percent(age) of rehabilitation in global adjustment." In another group, consisting of narcotic addicts, many reported the LSD/music therapy as creating a "confrontation with their problems, rather than an escape" (Pahnke et al. 1970, p. 1859).

Gaston and Eagle, who participated in the Kansas study with LSD/music, reported that all therapists agreed that music was an essential element of LSD treatment (Gaston and Eagle 1970). The purpose of the music, according to Helen Bonny, was:

1. to help the patient relinquish usual controls and enter more fully into his inner world,
2. to facilitate the release of intense emotionality,
3. to contribute toward a peak experience,
4. to provide continuity in an experience of timelessness,
5. to direct and structure the experience (Bonny and Pahnke 1972, 66).

Though the therapists in Maryland and Kansas all agreed that music was essential to the LSD/music therapy, Helen Bonny recognized that the LSD was not. With the MPRC research as a departure point, and incorporating the work of Leuner, Bonny developed a technique of humanistic therapy for work with "normal" people. "People," Bonny explains, "who were on the quest for self-actualization. Already relatively healthy, they were seeking fuller experience and insight in the areas of the humanistic, and transpersonal" (Bonny 1980, 25). In the early 70s, Bonny was in the avant garde of mental health professionals who were just then recognizing the value of increased self awareness and perception, even in the mentally healthy population.

Working with groups of normal individuals, Bonny constructed the technique now known as Guided Imagery and Music. As in the MPRC research, a GIM session began with a pre-session conducted in a normal state of consciousness in which Bonny would describe the forthcoming itinerary of the session. Alleviated of questions and uncertainty about the session, the participants would then be open to experiencing an altered state of consciousness. To replace the LSD, that had been so successful in creating that altered state of consciousness, Bonny drew on the relaxation techniques of Jacobsen and Schultz. With bodies relaxed and minds open, one of the ten Leuner inductions was said in preparation for the music. Using music proven effective with the MPRC subjects under the influence of LSD, Bonny discovered that the use of relaxation and induction in place of LSD served equally well in producing dynamic imagery. A post-session in which Bonny and the participants reviewed the imagery was conducted in the fashion of Leuner, but differed in that, whereas Leuner drew conclusions directly from the imagery, Bonny allowed the participants to draw their own conclusions. Bonny's humanistic application of Leuner's psychoanalytic technique culminated in the development of the individual GIM session.

Departing from Leuner's directive guiding, Bonny viewed the professional therapist component of the therapist-patient dyad as a facilitator, a support for the self-actualization process.

In "Music Therapy: A Legal High," Bonny defines GIM as "a technique which involves listening to music in a relaxed state to elicit imagery, symbols and/or feelings for the purpose of creativity, therapeutic intervention, self understanding and religious (spiritual) experience" (Bonny and Tansill 1977, 113–114).

In 1972 Bonny founded the Institute for Consciousness and Music for the purpose of refining, furthering research, and training professionals in the use of GIM with normal clients, under her stewardship. In 1986 she left the helm of ICM and founded Music Rx, continuing her work in the field of music and altered states of consciousness.

During her tenure at ICM, the group GIM session was used primarily to introduce future practitioners to the technique of the GIM individual session. With the exception of this group teaching session, the potential use of GIM in groups was not explored at ICM.

FOUR

GIM: PRELUDE

We say of course that music "addresses itself to the ear"; but it does so only in a qualified way, only in so far, namely, as the hearing, like the other senses, is the deputy, the instrument, and the receiver of the mind. Perhaps, said Kretschmar, it was music's deepest wish not to be heard at all, or even seen, nor yet felt: but only—if that were possible—in some Beyond, the other side of sense and sentiment, to be perceived and contemplated as pure mind, pure spirit.
—from *Doctor Faustus* by Thomas Mann

The group GIM session begins with the prelude. The therapist addresses each group member with direct and simple dialogue, describes the GIM procedure thoroughly, and delineates the specific goals for the session. No music is used during the prelude. The group members do not converse amongst each other nor establish links of any kind. Rather, the therapist emphasizes the individual nature of the GIM experience. (In the postlude the group interacts.)

In a typical prelude, exemplified by "Give and Take," which took place at a psychiatric hospital, I began by suggesting the group form a circle on the floor, "Find yourself a comfortable pillow and sit down in a circle. I know you've had psychodrama this morning. Let's find out how each of you are feeling." Rather than wait for an individual to volunteer, I turned to a patient named Oliver and asked if he had "any feelings left from this morning's group."

"That stuff about Dick's mother really got to me. I can't believe someone's mother would really do that stuff we acted out."

"What's your feeling when you think about that?" I asked.

"It makes me worry about my relationship with my son. I hate hurting him."

"So, you're thinking about your son?"

"Yeah."

"And you feel worried?"

"Yeah."

"Thanks for telling us, Oliver. Let's go on to Mac."

As with Oliver, I conducted a brief questioning with Mac, and subsequently with each group member. I noted that Dick was the focus of the morning's psychodrama session, and that a number of the group members were identifying with him. Addressing the group as a whole I suggested to those who were thinking about the morning session, "Let yourself bring the feelings into this music session, rather than the actual content of the scene Dick played out this morning. If you still have those feelings you don't need to ignore them here, but we're not going to be dealing with those same issues. We've gone around the circle; it's interesting to see how differently you each feel. Now, most of you have had GIM sessions before, and today's will be similar in many ways to our previous ones. We're going to have an adventure with music. First we're going to get relaxed with some deep breathing. I'll put on some taped music that will last about five minutes. The object is not to listen to the music, but to explore what the music brings up in you. Use the time during the music to explore, really explore. The music will suggest an experience to you. If the music sounds sad, it might remind you of something sad; someone in your life, or a place. It might sound happy, like dancing or flying. Whatever the music seems to tell you to do or experience, you can do. There are no restrictions since you're using your imagination. You CAN fly. You can swim underwater without need for air, and the music can even help you to imagine something that you have never before thought about. I want to encourage you to be adventurous with this music."

"I'd like to suggest an issue that has to do with our community here. When we're part of a group there is always give and take. For just a moment think to yourself, what is it that you get from this community? What is it that you give to others? Is there a specific person in this group who helps you, quite a bit? Are there certain situations when you need help in which you find yourself thinking about this group? And are there situations in which you particularly like being a part of this group? After you are lying down and relaxed I will help you again to focus on these issues prior to the music coming on. After the music is over we'll get up and discuss."

"Give and Take," as can be seen from this excerpt of the prelude, was used to help these group members increase their ability to offer and receive support, to gain access to unacknowledged positive aspects of the self, to increase openness to new experiences, and to expand coping skills for daily life problems. I also used this activity to strengthen the group support system.

Though in a group session the prelude focuses upon a specific goal, there can be no such specific objective in a prelude for an individual. In GIM, which is after all a humanistic therapy, it is desirable to allow the client to guide his own therapy as much as possible, making it inappropriate to focus too much upon a therapist's goal. However, it would be equally inappropriate, if not more so, to give the members of the group free rein in an altered state while listening to music because the diversity of experiences in an unfocused group GIM session would undermine the rationale for the group itself.

GIM is often conducted serially. The previous example, "Give and Take," is in fact taken from a series of GIM sessions with a group on a short-term high functioning neurotic unit at a psychiatric hospital. The clients came and went at various times within the series but much like a symphony orchestra where members come and go, the group maintains an identifiable sound, new members finding their niche within the ever evolving ensemble.

Regardless of the number of GIM sessions a group has had, the prelude always retains a thorough explanation of the GIM technique.

FIVE

GIM: RELAXATION AND INDUCTION

I ordered my horse to be brought from the stables. The servant did not understand my orders. So I went to the stables myself, saddled my horse, and mounted. In the distance I heard the sound of a trumpet, and I asked the servant what it meant. He knew nothing and had heard nothing. At the gate he stopped me and asked: "Where is the master going?" "I don't know," I said, "just out of here, just out of here. Out of here, nothing else, it's the only way I can reach my goal." "So you know your goal?" he asked. "Yes," I replied, "I've just told you. Out of here—that's my goal."
—from *Departure* by Franz Kafka

Relaxation

Relaxation techniques vary according to the goals of the specific GIM session. In one group activity, the "Ideal Self" session, the clients imagined what they would like to look like in five years. In order to facilitate this goal the relaxation technique was more involved than usual. It began with a stretching exercise. "Let's stand up, as straight as you can make yourselves," I addressed the group. "Imagine that you are standing against a wall. Take a quick deep breath, and let it out very slowly. Now watch me and when I'm done we'll do this one together. Starting at the top you are going to fold down. I drop my chin onto my chest, feeling it's weight, my shoulders hunch forward, my arms hang loose and so do my fingers, I bend at the waist, keeping my knees bent also." I led the group in the preceding exercise. When this was complete I continued, "Now that we are down here, allow any tension you feel inside to be drawn out, as if by gravity down your body and out your arms and fingers, and your legs and toes...and your head and your hair. Shake your head gently, and your arms. Shake off any tension...shake off that tension. Now we'll come up slowly just reversing what we did. Begin by straightening your waist, now your shoulders, now your head. Take a slow deep breath in, and a fast one out. We'll do this again two more times."

After the group had repeated the exercise twice I asked them to lie down, "making yourselves comfortable on the floor with your pillow. Close your eyes, and let's do some deep breathing. You can just follow along with my instructions. I will count for you from 1 to 8 and you can just follow along with my counting. Now, exhale all of your air...and inhale, 2, 3, 4, 5, 6, 7, 8. Exhale, 2, 3, 4, 5, 6, 7, 8." The deep breaths were repeated, becoming slower with each repetition, five more times after which I suggested the clients' breathing return to a normal, comfortable pace.

Though the relaxation technique should take away any superficial tension that the clients have in their bodies to put them in a receptive mode for the music to come, the goal of the relaxation portion is not to confront the deeply embedded tensions that are a part of the individual's psychological make up. Indeed, if a relaxation technique could alleviate chronic physiological problems by itself there would be little need for most forms of therapy. In dealing with groups in which chronic pain or illness is a feature it is wise to state clearly the function of the relaxation portion of the session to understand that relaxation is not a goal of the session. Various types of relaxation exercises work in GIM. Helen Bonny, in *Facilitating GIM Sessions*, refers to Jacobsen's Progressive Relaxation, and Schultz and Luthe's Autogenic Training. In fact, there are many effective techniques, most of which use a juxtaposition of tension and relaxation or various deep breathing exercises.

When working with an individual the client is encouraged to relax to a greater extent and the therapist is able to work with specific parts of the client's body which are more tense than others. In fact, in order to allow for a deeper altered state of consciousness than is achieved by individuals during a group session, a more extensive relaxation technique is necessary. This longer relaxation minimizes ego defenses allowing the music to elicit material from deeper within the client's unconscious. This is achieved through the simple method of addition. Rather than counting from one to eight, one counts to ten, increases the number of breaths taken, and slows down the counting. A sensitive therapist will be able to isolate parts of the client's body that need specific attention.

Induction

The relaxation technique having lessened the domination of the brain's left hemisphere, the induction serves as a stimulus for the right hemisphere. Focusing upon a specific image, the induction gives a goal toward which to work in the music/imagery synergy. The therapist encourages creativity, adventure and risk taking and directs the client into the experience of the music. Peach (1984) aptly describes an induction as specific imagery encouraging multiple sensory involvement.

There are two parts to the induction: the image and the goal. A visual image is chosen by the therapist for the client in order to symbolize a part of the client's self. The goal, also chosen by the therapist in order to aid the client in attaining personal growth, is successfully realized if and when the client is able to synergize the goal with the visual image.

With another group of high functioning neurotics at a psychiatric hospital the image of an island was used for the induction. In the prelude I posed questions about "acceptance." The group considered who in their lives was most accepting of them. For the imagery my clients were instructed to "bring along one 'accepting' person," care being taken that the choice did not involve someone unavailable to that person, such as someone deceased. A simple relaxation technique was used, following which I began the induction.

"If you have any thoughts on your mind, allow them to become less and less important. Your thoughts can become less important, fading further and further away. Fading away, further and further into the distance, so that your mind becomes more and more clear, more and more open. Allowing your thoughts to fade away, allowing your mind to become more and more open, allowing yourself to focus upon the person whom you have chosen to bring with you. Imagine the two of you together. What are you wearing? How do you look? Look at your faces. Notice the feeling of being with them. Allow yourself now to imagine a boat. The boat is anchored next to the shore of a river. You can see it rocking gently with the small waves. Let the two of you get into the boat, for a short trip. The boat will take you to an island which you can see in the distance. You will travel gently to the island, and when you arrive there you can anchor the boat and go exploring. During the music, let yourself experience the feelings of being on the island with this person. One of you may find that there is something on the island to bring back with you. As the music ends I will help you get back into your boat and return."

In my effort to clarify the clients' support system, increase their ability to receive support, facilitate communication between aspects of the self (the accepting part and its opposite), to mobilize inner strength, and to increase responsibility to oneself I used the image of the island combined with the "accepting person" to "find something": the goal.

Were I to use this induction with an individual rather than a group the only alteration in its presentation would be the directive concerning action, i.e., "find something on the island to bring back with you." Suggesting goals during the induction in individual session is counterproductive as well as futile since the client is apt to disregard exterior boundaries when in a deeper altered state of consciousness. For an individual, the preceding induction would end, "During the music let yourself experience the feelings of being on the island with this person, and allow it to show you an experience there."

In my work with the elderly I realized that in groups in which many newcomers to the GIM experience are present it is wise to offer images as immediate and specific as possible. For example, when using the island induction described above, I would exhibit an enlarged photo of a boat docked at a shore with an island in the distance; thus offering a concrete image upon which to focus (Summer 1981a).

A unique type of induction for groups is one in which a group image is formed. In one instance in my work with substance abusers I introduced an empty chair to the group (Perls 1974). The group created a figure in the chair by contributing adjectives to describe an imaginary person, the only guideline given being that this imaginary person was an alcoholic. The group described physical features such as hair color, height, clothing, and some overt emotional attributes which could be perceived by looking at the imaginary person. I allowed each client to contribute an element of the description in turn until a complete picture was created. After a summary, the character was dubbed Al Cohol. I began the induction to the GIM experience by describing the Al Cohol that the group created. "Where is he? Allow yourself to really see him," I continued, "I invite you to let yourself be there with Al and to allow the music to suggest a way to be with him, or interact with him. The music will suggest an experience to you, so allow it to come with you and Al." In this induction I used the image of Al as the alcoholic part of the self, the goal being to interact or confront it.

SIX

GIM: MUSIC/IMAGERY SYNERGY, POSTLUDE, AND GUIDING

An amusing head on collision between two computer programs, ("Doctor" created by Joseph Weizenbaum simulating a psychiatrist using "nondirective therapy," and "Parry," created by Kenneth Colby to simulate the belief structure of a paranoid) was arranged over a computer network and the following is a short excerpt from the full transcript.

Parry:	*I don't understand your motives.*
Doctor:	*Why don't you understand my motives?*
Parry:	*Should I be?*
Doctor:	*Why do you say that just now?*
Parry:	*That's just the way it is.*
Doctor:	*Suppose that's just the way it were not.*
Parry:	*So?*
Doctor:	*I am not sure I understand you fully.*
Parry:	*You harp on the same questions too much.*
Doctor:	*What does that similarity suggest to you?*
Parry:	*I don't get you.*
Doctor:	*Do you wish that you did get I?*
Parry:	*It's about time you showed some interest in my feelings.*
Doctor:	*Oh? I showed some interest in your feelings?*

—from *Godel, Escher, Bach* by D. R. Hofstadter

Music/Imagery Synergy

At the core (or coeur) of GIM is the music/imagery synergy portion. All the preparations have been pointed towards this ineffable marriage of music and the psyche. No one doubts the unique relationship of music to the soul though it is with great difficulty that this relationship can be defined. A painting may move us to tears because of its subject but rarely because of its beauty. Likewise with poetry or prose we admire and enjoy most a great author but can be moved to tears by a mediocre author when the subject matter is something universally poignant. In music there are parallel cases, such as the painful association with a specific piece in which we may find ourselves, for instance, in tears because a song reminds us of a broken romance. (Sad lyrics that evoke tears are more in the realm of the literary tearjerker, though a literary tearjerker in the hands of a skilled musician may cause the most embittered cynical person to cry, such as my husband's reaction to La Boheme, a text which he deplores as being trivial.) But how can we explain the tears and emotional overflowing evoked by totally abstract music? What makes one cry during the development of Mozart's *Jupiter Symphony's* last movement or bawl during even a mediocre performance of the third movement of Beethoven's *Ninth* or moan audibly during the slow movement of Mahler's *Sixth*? How can one explain the mirth and true laughter evinced by so many Haydn symphonies and string quartets or the feeling of inner fortitude created upon listening to Bach's *Brandenburg Concerto No. 1*? Every subtlety of emotion is evoked at one time or another by great music. Yet this "great music" can only be defined by naming the composers who wrote it. What makes Mozart Mozart and Salieri Salieri? The notes? They are the same. The chord progressions? There is not one chord progression in Mozart that is not duplicated exactly in Salieri. The choice of instruments? The same. There are no objective factors to which we can point as defining great music, yet we know in our heart because those composers who have succeeded in writing great music are those composers who have found the emotional corollary in pure sound to our soul.

Music therapists need be aware that, unlike any other therapy, ours has the closest link to the subconscious. Great art is always attempting to reach the subconscious, but before it can reach it, it must perforce define an object or situation. A great novel that moves us defines a situation that evokes emotion. A great poem defines a situation that evokes emotion. A great work of visual art though supplying us with less information about a situation encourages us to flesh out the story. (In *Guernica* our emotional response to the art is instructed to us by Picasso through the understanding of the deaths involved in an incident.) Even in abstract art we look for a parallel in the concrete world. A specific piece may "look" like a waterfall and carry with it implications for ourselves but, nevertheless, we have translated the visual image again into an incident or situation that has a concrete reference in the "real world." Dance, when not telling a specific story, still informs us of physical processes which are a part of our concrete world. On the other hand music has no "real world" referents. Sibelius' *Second Symphony* doesn't *mean* anything. It doesn't stand for a physical aspect of the external world. It evokes emotions isotropically. It is poignant, when it is poignant, because Sibelius intended it to be poignant; not because it refers to any "thing" poignant. Because pure music has no verbal referents it can hurdle the left hemisphere, finding itself in the right, speaking to us in the language of emotions. (There is of course music that does contain referents to the real world; opera, ballet music, and programmatic pieces, though even these when separated from their verbal or physical context can have the same effect as abstract music and are used occasionally in GIM. For instance the knowledge of German would make the use of Brahms' *German Requiem* unsuitable for GIM because of its explicit meaning, whereas with the absence of the knowledge of German it can be used as a nonreferential piece.)

When doing GIM on a group basis it is not desirable to eliminate the defenses and all references to reality. This is the reason for a brief and superficial relaxation technique and for specific and restricted guidelines used during the induction for the visual image and goal setting. It is only by working through his defenses and reality referents in the form of an induction that an unhealthy individual is able to be aided in therapy by the language and wisdom of the emotions contained in the right hemisphere. Most importantly, there is no guiding during the music/synergy portion of the GIM session for groups, where there is guiding of the individual because, contrary to expectations, guiding during the music/imagery synergy actually increases the depth of the experience. With a guide present during the music the client feels safer to explore the subconscious and will do so. In the absence of that guide, as in the group sessions, the clients will not be able to venture into territory better left for healthy individuals to explore.

Postlude

Guiding for the group occurs in the postlude after the music is over. The postlude of the group GIM session returns the clients to their normal verbal mode by easing them back into the "real world." This return to normal consciousness is accomplished through a reversal of the relaxation/induction techniques. For example, in the postlude to the previously mentioned session wherein the induction involved visiting an island with an accepting person, I said, as the music was ending, "Allow yourself to return to the shore of the island to find your boat anchored there at the shore. Allow yourself to bring back anything you have found there—it need not actually fit in the boat. After you are comfortably inside the boat, let it take you gently and directly back to your starting place. As you leave the island your awareness will bring you back more and more to where you started, and back to this room. Coming back more and more…coming back more and more to the room. Feel your back on the floor, and remember where you are in the room. As you are ready, open your eyes and sit up in your place."

Following the clients' reemergence, the therapist requests a report of each client's imagery experience during the music, followed by a discussion with the group; in order first, to apply the imagery experience to each client's current life or goals in therapy and secondly, to work toward group goals.

The experience of imagery to music, as in a dream, often fades away if it is not made conscious. Therefore it is very important for the therapist to encourage each client to first report their experience fully without interruption from other group members. In a GIM session with a group of alcoholics and drug addicts, in which prior to the music experience each group member drew a picture of an animal, each member during the postlude was instructed to write ten adjectives on the back of their drawing describing their music experience. I began by asking John what the music suggested to him.

"Well," he said, "when you said to be the dog, I did.[1] I was sneaking around in my yard and my neighbors' yards."

"What did you do?"

"I was just eating, looking for other animals, getting through fences I wasn't supposed to be getting through."

"After further questioning he added,

"Urinating, you know. That's what dogs do."

In order to "ground" the client's experience the therapist and the group help the client explore his imagery, finding logical relationships in structure and content between the imagery experience and actual life.

After John had talked about the basic "facts" of his imagery, I interrogated him further with an eye towards the goals of the session, i.e., the depiction, verbalization, and acceptance of an aspect of the self for the purpose of the identification of weaknesses, strengths, and patterns of behavior. I asked him what adjectives he had written down to describe his experience. "Sleek, tricky, alert, tough, watchdog, black and white, controlled, lonely, easy, simple—that's what it was like to be a dog," he told us.

"When you were the dog, did you feel like John or did you feel very different?"

"The way the dog was, that's not how my life is now. I have so many responsibilities. I worry about my finances. Dogs don't need money in the bank, just some food and a place to urinate."

Reflecting his comments I responded,

"It's different from your life now?"

---

[1]N.B. I did not instruct the client to 'be a dog.'

"Yes, except the tricky way he got what he wanted by just sneaking it."

"Tell us about that."

"Well, during the music I was frisky and running around the neighborhood. I was by myself and very small. I could sneak around people's houses and backyards without getting caught. I could take anything I wanted without getting caught. It was so easy. The dog's life is so simple and predictable. I didn't have to worry or think about anything. I think I'd like a dog's life. They really have it easy."

In group therapy of any kind the group itself acts as therapists for the individual members. As Fine (1979, 429) so aptly expresses it, "Each patient is the therapeutic agent of the other." In the postlude to the GIM experience once the individual, with the aid of the therapist, has described their experience the group as a whole is invited to comment. In John's case, following our dialogue, the group confronted John about his isolation on the unit, his attempts to avoid group therapy sessions, and the reason for his being on the unit; namely, his drinking.

Elliot, another alcoholic in the group, shared later. During the imagery session Elliot had pictured himself as an eagle, though able to fly for only a short time. He became confused, he explained, and landed on a plateau, unmoving, for the rest of the music. "I know how John felt," Elliot remarked at one point during his narrative.

During the integration part of the postlude I asked Elliot about his identification with John.

"Elliot, you mentioned when you were sharing that you understood how John felt in his imagery...."

"Well, I know how he feels about...looking around for other animals."

"Tell us about that."

"It's not as obvious with me because I'm so friendly; but I haven't *really* talked to anyone on this unit since I got here. It's been three days."

Addressing the group, I asked if anyone could see anything that could be done to help both John and Elliot. Thereafter followed a discussion in which most of the group members participated making suggestions and comments.

In a series of GIM sessions with a group the therapist becomes familiar with the members' progress (or lack thereof) and guides the postlude through whatever questioning is necessary for each individual. Integrating the group in an exciting way provokes new learning and deeper relationships among the group members.

Comparisons between material and behavior from past sessions is an excellent indicator of progress. In a subsequent GIM session with John, (the alcoholic who had imagined himself as a dog,) the group members were directed to imagine an alcoholic (using the Al Cohol induction previously described). In John's imagery Al Cohol reflected the sneaky, simple, easy personality of his dog. Al Cohol tried to trick him into buying and sharing a bottle of whiskey with him. Seeing through his trickery John was able to refuse the drink. In the postlude John quickly recognized the similarity between the character of the dog and Al Cohol, thus addressing this aspect of himself.

Guiding

Whereas in group GIM sessions the guiding occurs during the postlude, in individual sessions guiding takes place during the music/imagery synergy. In "Music therapy: A legal high," Helen Bonny states that guiding is, "a close interactional one to one communication, in which an inward-outward flow of nonstatic personal material is amplified by music-evoked imagery, becoming crystallized at intervals by concrete verbal statements and descriptions. The therapist uses confrontation, Gestalt, bioenergetics, role play, and stream of consciousness to encourage exploration once an important area has been reached" (Bonny and Tansill 1977, 121).

The purpose of guiding is to stimulate imagery and to stimulate involvement in imagery. These two purposes are identical to the purpose of using music because in Guided Imagery and Music, the music therapist is co-therapist with the music. While the music is playing the client reports his imagery verbally. This verbalization increases the client's ability to imagine.

During the music the guide has four primary responsibilities. First, the therapist asks for description. This encourages the imagery to take on a sharper form moving it forward, and stimulating involvement thus faciliating the creation of further imagery. Second, the therapist encourages involvement in the imagery, prompting the client to investigate through different perspectives; not just seeing the image of an ocean, but perhaps seeing it from a closer viewpoint, or smelling it. The therapist encourages the client to become more active in the experience as well, such as descending into the ocean or transforming the ocean into something else. Third, the therapist reflects the imagery, thereby supporting what the client is experiencing. Fourth, throughout the music the therapist helps the client to focus on the music, allowing the music to direct the experience. This focus allows the client's psyche to remain in a nonverbal, nondefensive mode; preventing the client from logically rationalizing how the imagery will evolve.

The following excerpt is from a GIM session with Fawn, a 23-year-old healthy female client.[2] After a brief discussion in this, Fawn's sixth session, the client lay supine on a mat on the floor. When the music started, "Siegfried's Funeral March" from Wagner's *Götterdämmerung*, Fawn said,

> "Everything is black. It's dark. There is a feeling of expectation in the music. I feel like something is going to happen."

> Focusing on the music, I said, "Let the music suggest what might happen."

> "The black is in my way. The music sounds angry. I can't see past the black."

> "Tell me about the black," I requested, to prompt a description.

> "It's like velvet and very thick and heavy. It's immense, it's suffocating.... It's like a giant octopus, the way it is all around me."

> "It's all around you?" I asked, reflecting.

> "It won't get out of my way. It's making me angry. Any way I turn it's there. It's an immense octopus, and the tentacles are barring my way. I can't find a way around it. I'm getting really mad...I am furious at the octopus and want to kill it."

> Hoping to stimulate her involvement, I asked, "Where do you feel the anger?"

---

[2]The excerpts from Fawn's case study appeared in L. Summer (1985a), Imagery and music. I have expanded upon the article with explanatory comments and further session material.

"It's in my arms and legs. I want to stomp on the octopus and smash it."

Encouraging deeper involvement through action I said, "Can you do that?"

"I can, but I don't think that will kill it. I have to smash each tentacle to stop it."

"Let the music help you."

"Yes, the music gives me energy. I am stomping it with the loud beats. I'm getting the first tentacle...."

"In guiding," writes Sara Jane Stokes, "it is necessary to create a healing environment through a special quality called 'presence.' There is constant interaction of unspoken thought and feeling going on between therapist and client. Healing involves the conscious and focused interaction of these energy fields within a person and also between the healer and patient" (Stokes 1985, 23–24).

Rider states that imagery must occur naturally and spontaneously in one's own mind. "Overguiding is commonly found on many "new age" recordings oriented towards stress reduction and behavioral medicine populations"(Rider 1987, 117).

The postlude for the individual is identical in purpose and structure to that of the group postlude with the notable exceptions that (1) imagery is not reported as it has been reported during the music experience and (2) there is not group interaction. In work with normal clients, it is common to incorporate artwork in the postlude. Carol Bush, who uses GIM in private practice, relies heavily on the symbology of mandalas. Her clients, in the postlude, either draw mandalas or choose one of twenty six mandala cards designed by Joan Kellogg.[3] Bush states, "The mandala as a circular art form, is an archetypal symbol representing wholeness." Mandalas drawn in the sessions are interpreted on the basis of color, movement, and symbols (Bush 1988, 2).

In the postlude to Fawn's sixth GIM experience, Fawn grappled with the image of the octopus. After assisting her back to a normal state of consciousness I asked Fawn how she was feeling.

"I feel really tired, but really good. That was exhausting work. I feel like I really did something there."

"What is it that you did?"

"Well, that suffocating feeling...at first I was powerless against it, but then...well...it felt like something that needed doing but at first, I didn't think I could."

"You didn't think you could?"

"Yeah, I felt really defeated."

"Tell me about that defeated feeling."

"I'm always getting defeated, so I guess that's why I feel it. Whenever I fight, I can't seem to direct my anger so that it does any good. I just get mad, and then lose. Sometimes I'm right, too, but I always lose anyway."

---

[3]Joan Kellog developed the Mari Card Test—a set of design cards and color cards developed from symbols and colors and bits of information found over time to be embedded in mandalas made by subjects in clinical and research settings.

"Can you think of a time like that?"

"Yes, my mother called me this week and asked me to do something for her. I got really mad at her because that wasn't really what she wanted. But, instead of fighting her, I just ended up hanging up the phone."

"What was that feeling like?"

"Defeated, and really mad."

"Does your imagery say anything to you regarding this?"

"Yes, I think that if I would have stayed on the phone and engaged in the fight, like I did with the octopus, it would have been better."

"How so?"

"Well, just like smashing each tentacle, I could smash her reasons for wanting me to go with her. If I smashed each one in turn, then she wouldn't have anything left to fight with."

"Is that something you'd like to try?"

"Yes."

"Let's talk about that further."

Following this discussion about possible methods of coping with her dilemma the GIM session was concluded.

SEVEN

GIM WITH THE INDIVIDUAL

I saw an ample moat bent like a bow,
    As one which all the plain encompasses,
    Conformable to what my Guide had said.

And between this and the embankment's foot
    Centaurs in file were running, armed with arrows,
    As in the world they used the chase to follow.

Beholding us descend, each one stood still,
    And from the squadron three detached themselves,
    With bows and arrows in advance selected;

And from afar one cried: "Unto what torment
    Come ye, who down the hillside are descending?
    Tell us from there; if not, I draw the bow."

—from *The Inferno* by Dante

Through the inferno to the gates of Paradise, Virgil guides the pilgrim, Dante. This is no group tour and Dante relies heavily on the reassuring presence of Virgil. When GIM is practiced with institutionalized psychiatric clients, the guide must be able not only to show the way into the inner circles of the psyche, but also the way back to the surface. Institutionalized psychiatric clients have weaknesses in ego structure which necessitate a therapeutic approach that uses clear boundaries and stresses cause and effect. In my work with these special clients I first created sessions in which each component was focused upon a highly defined purpose much in the same way as I did my group sessions. However, even with a very structured prelude, relaxation/induction, guiding during the music/imagery synergy and postlude; the client's psyche responds to the combination of a supportive guide, classical music, and altered state of consciousness with the natural tendency to produce imagery material of its own agenda. A wealth of unconscious material often surfaces irrevocably and the symbolism of the imagery requires of the therapist an immense effort to help "ground" it.

When dealing with Fawn, for example, it was easy for Fawn to make a connection between the imagery of the octopus and the reality of her mother. The ease of transition between the imagery of the psyche and the reality of the external world is not necessarily duplicated with the institutionalized client. The inability to reconcile internal and external reality is usually the very reason that the client is in a hospital.

Because GIM allows the client to move at his own rate, if the illness is a severe emotional one, the rate is often too slow for short-term inpatient work. Casey is an example of this.

Casey,[1] a 56-year-old white male, diagnosed as having recurrent major depression, with compulsive defenses and subsurface paranoia, had attempted suicide and was brought to a

---

[1]Casey's case study was also reported in L. Summer & N. Roby (1981), Reaching the addictive personality through imagery, art and music.

private psychiatric hospital. He had been hospitalized three times previously, had been going to Alcoholics Anonymous for twenty years, and was reportedly twenty years sober. Married in his 20s for eight years and then divorced, Casey drank heavily during this period. He had used alcohol to attempt suicide several times, and at the time of the therapy was addicted to Librium. Prior to hospitalization he was unemployed. Twice weekly for six weeks he participated in 1.5 hour group GIM sessions. During that period he had eight half hour individual GIM sessions. Casey was very verbose, but irrelevant in his prolixity. The staff and I agreed that he had been trying to "split the staff."

Casey's noted prolixity resulted in session notes several times longer than any other client's in which he would describe every aspect of the imagery that the music elicited. His imagery included intense scenes and feelings which would disintegrate, evanesce, dissolve, integrate into photograph-like two dimensional pictures, and turn black and white. Concurrently he would report vivid physical sensations such as a feeling of floating, a very dry mouth, and intense discomfort in his eyes.

He described "The Light" as an inward lighting, persistent, consuming, revelatory, nourishing, cold, flaming albescent, primal, and powerful. Sometimes the light was like a silk sheet, sometimes a yellow and orange cold light, and sometimes a raining light or even a waterfall. In nearly all of his sessions he experienced various manifestations of "The Light." His encounters with "The Light" were in the form of a quest, always hindered by buildings and shells of buildings, "empty" hospitals, rotten desiccated places, barren lands, caverns lined with bones, flat gray blocks, geometric lines, and various impenetrable surfaces. His perception of the music itself was also characterized by images, one notable description equating music with an immense steel turbine.

These very vivid images always metamorphosed before he could act upon them. Notwithstanding the vivid imagery, Casey showed little involvement or activity in them throughout the sessions.

Even in his experiences of "The Light" Casey's deeper self was hidden from him by his defenses, his depression taking the shape of the various obstructions. Intellectual and compulsive as his profuse descriptions were, he allowed himself meager involvement in the experience itself. He himself never appeared in any of the imagery sessions. In fact, Casey never saw a human figure in all of his GIM sessions. In his last session he saw a mannequin, the first approximation of human life encountered on the tableau of his imagery.

Casey was deeply moved during each of his sessions, afterwards drawing sometimes several pictures or writing dialogues between himself and his images. The intensity of his experiences, however, yielded little in terms of change in Casey's behavior or overall feeling.

Apparent in his case, as an exemplar of clients who suffer from major depression, it takes a long time to evoke meaningful growth with the GIM technique. In a short-term psychiatric hospital, it is inappropriate to initiate GIM therapy even if the resultant polymorphous perverse imagery produced (and in Casey's case quite spectacularly reproduced in his drawings) is exciting or titillating to the therapist.

Peach (1984, 33), through an analysis of imagery of psychotics, neurotics, and normals, noted that "Subjects taking antidepressants were most receptive to different modes of imagery; they experienced each type (except taste) more frequently than any other drug group. In addition, they had the highest total imagery mode average, i.e., they experienced more types of imagery concurrently than any other drug group." Those who are depressed can have fantastic imagery; beautiful, fast moving, and intense. They are not, therefore, excellent candidates for imagery therapy, nor does the work proceed at a faster pace or at a higher quality because of this. Vivid or prolific imagery does not equal efficacy in treatment.

As previously discussed many institutionalized patients do not have the ego strength to "ground" or apply imagery to their current life. As symbols are brought up from the unconscious, the weak ego has difficulty mediating between imagery and outer reality; so clients may verbalize analogous life situations without actually affecting any positive behavioral changes.

Whereas Casey could not analogize, Nancy could, yet could not follow through with positive growth. Though her imagery provided her with many possible solutions to her problems, she was unable to apply any of the insights to help herself. Plain, thin, and sad looking, Nancy attempted a look of youthfulness in her dress. She had two children and was forty years old. A widow, Nancy had been living with Patrick, a man whom she had "really opened up to and trusted." He had left her precipitously, without notice. Nancy was in the hospital to deal with the loss of Patrick, to relieve depression, to be able to function again in the outside world, and to lessen her anger with (all) men. She was diagnosed as having a dysthymic disorder (neurotic depression). Twice weekly for five weeks she participated in group GIM sessions of 1.5 hour each. In addition, during those five weeks I gave her five half hour individual GIM sessions.

Her sessions were filled with reference to her splitting with Patrick. In a beautiful, lush meadow in which Nancy was alone she related, "Only I am there.... It hurts to look at it without anyone to tell. I can't go closer or even look at it." She imagined Patrick in his home with an object of hers in a shoe box which he would not open. She experienced herself in the dark box, saying, "If only he would open it, I'd show him."

Much of her imagery consisted of tedious repair work, such as repairing a tear in a wall by hand in one case, and in another repairing damage incurred by a devastating fire.

Of her depression, Nancy had a very vivid metaphorical image in which she imagined herself covered by a black, vinyl record, her head poking out of the hole in the center. She resented the record, she said, since it ran her life. When she was happy the happiness lay on top of the record. She added that the record helped her to be careful of people who lie, and that the record "couldn't let anything in until something comes out." In one experience she found herself unable to escape a crowd of agitated people. Though she could fly, she was too fearful of being "shot down" out of the sky to escape the situation.

Nancy was experiencing a pathological split between good and bad brought about by her anxiety over the loss of Patrick. In her imagery she projected the good part of her outside of herself: the meadow and the happiness on top of the record. The bad part of her she experienced as within herself: her rage at Patrick while in the box and the tear in the wall which she "owned" and had to fix. Her repair work was symbolic of building boundaries between parts of herself which she could not allow to merge. She had a need to contain the rage she felt, to keep it inside her so that it would not destroy the good part of her.

Though able to strengthen her boundaries in her GIM sessions, Nancy was unable to reclaim the "good" part of her which she kept outside of herself. What Nancy needed was therapy of a supportive nature which would enable her to regain her balance and then to progress to solving her problems. What she did in GIM was obsessively to perseverate in the construction of well crafted imagery that defined her dilemma. All the loving and intricate details of her imagery are for naught but our own aesthetic appreciation, if they cannot impel her towards a successful working through of her problems and eventual health. In short-term work with the neurotically depressed GIM may not be able to be of enough benefit to warrant inclusion in the treatment plan. In private practice or in long-term treatment the therapist will have the advantage of an unrestricted period in which to work with the defensive images of the dysthymic client.

That individual GIM sessions with substance abusers would be effective we might have guessed from Helen Bonny's pioneering work at Epoch House.[2] In a sense the music therapist substitutes GIM for addictive behavior and in so doing, creates a healthily evoked altered state of consciousness. (As of yet, I know of no case of a music "addict" performing armed robbery to get a fix of Mahler.)

Donna, an amphetamine abuser, the only woman on a twelve bed substance abuse in-patient hospital unit, had virtually no interpersonal relationships on the unit. Unable or reluctant to participate once being admitted to the hospital, she was making no progress towards dealing with her addiction. Small, dark, in her early 20s, Donna spoke (and briefly at that) only when spoken to in her various group therapies. If pressed, she would have an outburst and retreat to her room. Concurrent with four weeks of group GIM sessions (two sessions each week, each session lasting 1.5 hours) I conducted two individual GIM sessions of half hour duration. As she was with all staff at the hospital, she was suspicious of me; however, she was able to trust the music which allowed her to participate in the GIM session, as she had been previously unable to do in any other type of therapy.

In Donna's first session she experienced a tightness in her chest, and visualized a black sponge, "Feeding on energy, it takes over everything," she reported. Using the music as "good energy" she was able to drain the sponge of its liquid, remedying her discomfort.

In the postlude she averred that she would be able to use this imagery to help her control her defensive impulses which were preventing her from participating in her treatment. Before each succeeding group therapy session (and during, if necessary) she intended to imagine the black sponge, heavy with liquid and then consciously empty it of its contents until she felt comfortable. She felt this would counter her feelings of loss of control and prevent her from withdrawing. After that initial GIM session Donna was able to participate in all aspects of treatment on the unit.

I have found great success using GIM with alcoholics and drug addicts with one exception: in group sessions with substance abusers who have used hallucinogenic drugs.[3] GIM helped Donna in a situation where nothing else had, especially verbal therapy. Though she did not trust me, GIM allowed her enough freedom within the structure/support of the music to begin to recognize her resistance to treatment and indeed, to find a method to overcome that resistance.

Frequently GIM may have no direct positive influence upon a hospitalized client's immediate behavior, but may serve as a key for further therapeutic treatment. Gary, an overweight, quiet, 19-year-old, diagnosed as having an adjustment disorder with mixed disturbance of emotion and conduct, did not benefit directly from his imagery regarding his identified problem. His GIM sessions (three half hour individual sessions and six 1.5 hour group sessions over a period of three weeks) enabled Gary to focus on the issues with which he would need to work in other modes of therapy.

Gary was sent by his parents to a psychiatric hospital because of violent physical outbursts directed against his father.[4] He had been in a halfway house but was thrown out for violating the rules, and had subsequently left a day hospital program because, he said, "It was stupid." The youngest of four children, and appearing even younger than his 19 years, Gary

---

[2]Helen Bonny used GIM at Epoch House with substance abusers.
[3]This class of substance abuser tends to have very advanced levels of imagery. In individual sessions it is possible to use this to the advantage of the therapy, but in group sessions the lack of the direct stabilizing effect of the guiding therapist can cause problems.
[4]Gary's case study was also reported in L. Summer & N. Roby (1981), Reaching the addictive personality through imagery, art and music.

felt closest to one brother who had died a few years before Gary's admission to the hospital. Gary had never dated. He described his mother as a good conversationalist and his father as physically large and good natured, but easily angered. Both parents, he said, were "disciplinarians." His parents planned to move to a new home to which he was not invited. After discharge from a previous treatment where he was diagnosed as having a passive aggressive personality disorder, his hatred for his father led to a violent confrontation and a court commitment for 90 days. Gary reported using marijuana, amphetamines, and LSD since the ninth grade, but reported that it caused "no problems." He also drank, though characterized it as social drinking.

The goal and reason for his referral to individual music therapy was to deal with his passive aggressive behavior, in general, as well as during group therapy. He was alienating the staff. No one could even approach him.

During individual therapy, Gary's imagery had two distinct characteristics: passive and aggressive. His passive imagery consisted of experiences in which he felt very alone and powerless. He watched, not participating. He became caught up in his emotions and withdrew, denying any control over the experiences. Over and over again he felt the pain of being left by his father in favor of his deceased brother. He imagined many hospitals and fled from all of them. He vividly experienced his own death and that of his brother, and regressed to his youth.

Interspersed with these passive experiences were images of immense Roman armies, hunting, killing of animals, and other aggressive activities. In his militaristic imaginings he was very involved in the discharge of weaponry though he never actually visualized the enemy. After this type of imagery he would express good feelings, as he did after an explosive, undirected discharge in real life.

In one session when he attempted to deal with the helpless passive feelings, he found that whenever he tried to be active "the weight of my stomach keeps me back." The stomach and its relation to his obesity were tied in with his passivity, his need to "swallow his anger."

The imagery which brought up the death of his brother and his own death led to an important postlude in which he identified with his brother and indicated feelings of responsibility for his death. The imagery allowed him to discharge some of his aggression in fantasy, and then, in the postlude to identify the reality behind his anger and the need to learn how to mobilize his anger in an appropriate manner.

Following the GIM sessions, Gary began to participate in group therapy sessions more fully and to express his anger appropriately, in many cases, to the therapists and staff on his unit. In his last art therapy session the art therapist reported that he came early rather than late, and that he sat next to him rather than across from him. He spoke about his dead brother in the group. For the first time he drew an abstract, not a representational, picture; showing an increased ability to deal with "abstract" feeling. He also chose a therapy with which to continue after his discharge.

In Gary's case, though GIM was ineffective in reaching specific goals, it nevertheless provided a launching platform for his work in other therapeutic venues. Thus, even in a situation where GIM may not directly aid an individual it can be of value in laying the ground work for positive behavioral change.

In Gary's case the GIM evoked a great amount of imagery beyond the scope of the therapeutic goals. GIM can do this, and thus, GIM can be counterproductive to the desires of the music therapist in certain situations. Wylie and Blom reported a case in individual work with hospice patients in which the therapist experienced unmanageability of the client's imagery. When asked to imagine an outdoor scene the client imagined a graveyard and became anxious and fearful. This was contrary to the goals in therapy which were to help the client "control her cancer/pain" by directive guiding. At that point the therapist redirected the procedure, changing to an indoor scene, and emphasizing that the client had control of her thoughts and images. The therapist also chose other methods of limiting the therapy by using music listening with popular, familiar and preferred music, and music designed for relaxation and meditation (Wylie and Blom 1986). These limiting factors took their music and imagery sessions out of the realm of GIM and into a more directive approach.

EIGHT

LEVELS OF IMAGERY

Parsifal: *I hardly move,*
Yet far I seem to have come.
Gurnemanz: *You see, my son, time*
changes here to space.
—from *PARSIFAL* by Richard Wagner

Four levels of imagery mark the substance of the client's internal journey. This journey may proceed inward, but very little, the client circumambulating on the outer fringe of the first level, the abstract /aesthetic level. He may explore this realm fully, or feeling ready for a deeper penetration of the psyche, proceed to the second level, that of psychodynamic experiences. The penultimate level, that of the perinatal experience is frequently the furthest journey the client will make. It is the rare, and generally healthier, traveler who makes the trip to the final level of transpersonal experience.[1]

The abstract/aesthetic experience is characterized by visual and kinaesthetic imagery, an altered perception of reality, and a deep enjoyment of the music. Experiences may seem ordinary on the surface, yet enhanced by their emotional context. An object which in an unaltered state of consciousness would be described by the client simply, on this level may acquire attributes of beauty, sensuousness, comedy or other surreal properties.

Viewpoint may be distorted, such as experiencing a sense of smallness or viewing a scene from above. Tammy, a high functioning inpatient at a private psychiatric hospital with a borderline personality disorder, while listening to the second movement of the Haydn *Cello Concerto*, experienced a "blue, swirling around, gracefully. There's no pattern. White is coming in and intermingling, like taffy. It's interesting. Here comes red. It pushes out the blue and white…gone…I see orchestra players, the conductor, white sheets of music. I'm in the room, relaxing…ballerinas. They seem really big. Oh, I'm watching from underneath them. It's like I'm very small and I'm off to the side in a corner. One of the ballerinas is me. She is dancing with a man. I've never seen myself like this. She has no idea that she's being watched. She knows the music perfectly and her dancing is in exact time with the music. It's so natural."

Many clients report discovering a new dimension in listening to the music. The music may trigger an emotion or seem to resonate in a certain part of the body. Also common is the perception of "knowing the music" expressed by clients who may have never before heard classical music.

The difference in perspective which comes with the aesthetic level is, naturally, a great aid to problem solving. Often a client is stymied by a difficulty which, if approached from a different angle, could be ameliorated. That different angle of approach which is suggested by the GIM experience can also provide new insight for the solution of a behavioral problem. To

---

[1]These four levels of imagery are first clearly defined in S. Grof (1976), *Realms of the human unconscious.*

encourage this experience in the GIM session I often make use of the "Animal" induction (see Chapter 6) which specifically encourages seeing from another point of view.

An alcoholic on a substance abuse unit, James' experiences during GIM therapy illustrate another aspect of the abstract/aesthetic level (as well as the second and third level experiences which will be attended to subsequently). James' imagery included abstract, geometric designs and dynamic color changes; the colors representing different aspects of himself. In a session in which James listened to the second movement of the Haydn *Cello Concerto* (as had Tammy) he experienced being in a bright warm place with different colors all around him. When I asked him about the colors, he replied, "Light blue, a weird green, red, grayish blue, light purple, black." I asked if he noticed anything about the colors. "They flow and trade places," he told me, "roll about. I'm surrounded by them." I asked him to tell me more about them. "They are smooth on the outside. The darker ones are rougher and uneasy; the lighter ones, mellow and smooth. They blend—float with each other. They wouldn't seem the same apart." Having asked if there was anything to do there, he responded, "I would like to go into the light blue. I do, and feel happy. The green is coming and it seems to say, 'Don't try to change anything here.' I would like to control the green but I can't. I want to take it away, but they all, these shapes and forms, coexist together in this weird way. They wouldn't function in the same way if one was removed."

The second level, psychodynamic experience, consists of literal, repressed memories; experiences of conflicts (especially interpersonal); and insights regarding aspects of one's life as symbolized in the imagery. On this level clients frequently confront their primary relationships, such as their parents, through actual or symbolic imagery.

Considerably resistant to participating in treatment (as may be adduced by his imagery in the previously noted session in which the color green, representing his alcoholic self said, "Don't try to change anything here"), James used alcohol to repress his pain and guilt. In another session, to the *allegro* movement of Brahms' *Piano Concerto No. 2*, James reached the psychodynamic level of imagery.

> "I'm in an area of space. I'm floating, warm, not sure of it. I feel threatened, but will risk it because it seems peaceful. My hands and feet are numb, so are my armpits and lower legs. I'm floating down and the more I do the cooler it gets. I think I'm in water but I don't feel it.[2]

> "The bottom is a valley, a repressed area between two hills. I'm looking down and it's black and large. It's a black hole—it goes forever....

> "I see a bottle. It's clear—gold label with red and gold lettering. Jessica is there. I see myself too. It's when I hurt her with my drinking to avoid pain. I can't tell her I'm sorry. It's dead when I try to tell her. The bottle has a voice and calls. I want to stay with Jessica, I can just look at her. I'm fighting myself and it's painful. Deep down I just want to drink. I don't want to say I'm sorry. Saying I'm sorry will bring pain.... Now I don't have any communication with the bottle any more.

> "There is an object in the background. It is a face with hands covering it. It's afraid to look at something. He is very old, has grey hair. He doesn't want to be seen. I want to pull the hands away, but I might harm him.

---

[2]I have eliminated my responses to James during this excerpt from the session.

"A window came up and I lost it. It's a church with bars. Some people are ahead of me and I want to follow to get to see the face. I could get in through the door and windows, but I may not be able to come back through."

Somatic and existential experiences characterize the perinatal level. Birth, death, and rebirth, as well as awareness and memories of body trauma and disease are the essential elements of the somatic experience. The inevitability of death is the tenor of the existential experience. In James' only session in which he experienced perinatal imagery he began,

"In a meadow in the middle. The grass is short and green. A brook goes into a pond with woods surrounding it. It's fall, leaves are yellow, sky is blue with clouds and birds, it's mellow.... I'm by the pond, sitting watching the water. Birds sweep across, going with the music. It's comfortable and safe. I walk over the hill to another meadow. On top of the peak I look around. There are animals all around. They accept me as one of them. They won't let me touch them. I'm alone in the crowd, but not alone. I feel like a prancer. The animals took off—something's coming. It's not safe, but I'm curious. It's something big—a bear—he's proud, claiming the area. He wants to chase me, but won't come near. I want him to leave. I don't want to have to hide. I want him to be friendly with me. He can if I let him.... I don't think he's there....[3]

"I'm stuck. I feel like a zombie—no physical feeling. I need to get out of here.

"I'm being moved—I've been beaten. I feel pain all over me. It's a dull pain.

"I see a crack in the darkness—light is coming through. It brings some warmth. There is pain just in existing. It's a part of me I don't want to face. I can't find a way to get rid of it. It's been years.

"I've been moved. I feel a lot lighter now. Out of the dark. I want to stop moving and stay in the light. I feel numb, except for the pain. It's hard to return. I feel a weight has been lifted from my body. I'm stiff. I actually feel ready to move on. It feels brighter, but not too friendly. Is the music over?"

As well as reflecting perinatal level body trauma (in this case, a physical beating), James' imagery includes an experience of birth as made evident in his references to "I'm stuck.... I need to get out of here. I'm being moved.... I see a crack in the darkness...out of the dark," etc.

Clients often experience one aspect of themselves on different levels. For instance, James experiences the alcoholic part of himself on the abstract/aesthetic level as the color green, on the psychodynamic level as the covered face of the old man and as a bottle of alcohol, and on the perinatal level as an unfeeling zombie.

The transpersonal level is most often experienced in GIM as a peak experience. Grof defines a peak experience as involving an expansion or extension of consciousness beyond the usual ego boundaries and beyond limitations of time or space (Grof 1976). Expanding upon this definition, Maslow notes feelings of unity, sacredness, paradoxicality, ineffability, as well as the transcendance of time and space as conditions for peak experience. In addition, Maslow contends the peak experience is a deeply felt positive mood, questioning the boundary between objectivity and reality; and that the experience is transient followed by a change in attitude and behavior (Maslow 1971). When this depth of level is attained, imagery loses

---

[3]I have eliminated my responses to James during this excerpt from the session.

its ordinary personal meaning and acquires a symbology of the universal, collective unconscious mind. Objects are viewed archetypically, so that the sun equals masculinity, the moon equals femininity, and so forth.

In institutional settings transpersonal experiences during the GIM session are rare. In group GIM sessions, due to the limiting factor of the absence of the guide, they are practically nonexistent. In individual sessions a transpersonal experience might grow out of a situation in which a client is in conflict in his imagery, as a supranormal solution, like a deus ex machina. (In the Euripidean tragedy, *Hippolytus*, a father and son are locked in a cycle of insoluble mutual antagonism. As the son dies, a goddess arrives out of the sky and reconciles the two, a task otherwise impossible due to their own personal viewpoints. The goddess' arrival in ancient Greece was accomplished by a machine, hence; deus ex machina.)

In "Music Therapy: A Legal High," Bonny and Tansill reported that in J.'s fifth session J. "saw a large chain link fence with barbed wire along its top; beyond the fence was a dark void. He felt apprehensive then became quite frightened. He was able to open the previously locked gate and enter the frightful darkness. The dark void had a hard white floor and only a lone scrubby tree growing in the floor. J. reported feeling shaky and '…weird all over like a hellish creature…a Minotaur.' With the strength of the bull J. tore up the floor which constricted the tree and as the floor was torn away the tree began to grow. As it did the darkness dissipated and he removed the fence as the tree became a forest. He grew tired, became old and hunched over. He died peacefully. He emerged from the grave as a skeleton and began to fill out into a complete body. He reported feeling smooth and supple as well as strong with catlike agility. He came upon a 'pale, white, translucent ovoid.' "

J., a former drug abuser, was drug abstinent when terminated from Epoch House in Baltimore where Bonny had worked with him. In addition, Bonny notes that his relationships with friends and parents improved after just his third session. J's significant improvement continued throughout the time he was monitored (one year following the end of therapy) (Bonny and Tansill 1977, 127–129).

After an extensive period of work on his addictive behavior at a psychiatric hospital, Ed, during group therapy, made a tremendous breakthrough. Following this breakthrough, during his second individual GIM session with me, he had a transpersonal experience thus granting himself a very useful healing experience.

> "I'm really afraid of what is ahead…very uncomfortable. It's really dark. I've stopped, I'm being scolded. There's a man above me, pointing down and mocking me for feeling sorry for myself and thinking bad thoughts, thoughts of pity. He says, 'It's self imposed. Just look around, you can think good things and you're using guilt….' "

Ed paused as the music of Glinka ended and Schubert's "Die Neugierige" from D*ie Schöne Müllerin* began.

> "The tone changed. He's finished berating me. I feel dejected, down, I've been stripped. It's a relief, I don't have to pretend and I can be on my way. A little hopeful. It's lighter. I feel like a child: clean, good; it's like I'm singing this song—sincerity, promise. I'm sorry for causing pain, but I had to be myself, to take chances…"

"Does this feeling have a color?" I asked him.

"Dazzling yellow."

"Can you surround yourself with it?"

"It's tingly, all around, in my heart, my soul."

"Is that where it needs to be?"

"All over, but I can't tell where my hands and feet are. I'm just experiencing this."

As "Die Neugierige" came to an end I asked Ed if he could say anything about his experience. He said, "No." I then asked him if he was ready to end with the music and he said he was.

The originators of psychedelic therapy used LSD to facilitate a therapeutic breakthrough which came in the form of a religious or mystical experience (Bonny and Pahnke 1972). They felt that the best level for therapy was the transpersonal level. In GIM the client is encouraged to work on the level he attains naturally and no steering towards a transpersonal level or any other level is appropriate.

On the abstract/aesthetic level insights and new experiences are stimulated. On this level the guide encourages visual description and exploration.

On the psychodynamic level defenses are elucidated and worked through, interpersonal conflicts are acted out and resolved in imagery, and solutions to life problems are found. On the psychodynamic level the therapist encourages involvement and interactions, catharsis of feelings, and problem solving.

Physical tensions are explored and relieved, and positive healing energies are activated on the perinatal level. The therapist focuses awareness on the body and upon any kinaesthetic or tactile imagery when working with a client on this level.

The transpersonal experiences unite the mind and body in a revelatory aura which transcends the boundaries of the other three levels in the quest of ultimate truths. It is not necessary for the guide to do much of anything on this level, except to give support and to allow the client a feeling of security in the guide's presence. Following a transpersonal experience it is very important to ground the client, bringing them back to outer reality and, regardless of the ineffability of the session, to process it.

Grof relates that in a series of music and imagery sessions with LSD it is usual to see a natural progression of levels from the aesthetic inward to transpersonal, but that special populations differ from the normal populations in that they do not usually take a direct route (Grof 1976). In group sessions with the populations discussed in this book it is most usual to see the abstract/aesthetic and psychodynamic levels. In individual sessions, there is occasionally a sojourn into the perinatal realm and, infrequently, into the transpersonal.

NINE

GIM-RELATED ACTIVITIES

Erda: My sleep is dreaming.
My dreaming meditation,
My meditation mastery of wisdom.
—from *Siegfried* by Richard Wagner

Whereas the use of the GIM technique is limited to those who have had formal training in the practice, for those who have not had this training there are GIM-like music listening exercises for use with groups.

The three examples mentioned below are also beneficial for the GIM-trained music therapist in introducing the GIM technique in groups in which it would be premature to begin the actual GIM experience. Common to all three is the format of the typical GIM session, i.e., prelude, relaxation, induction, music/imagery synergy, and postlude. All the preludes contain an explanation of the procedure of the exercise. Relaxation is limited to no more than a handful of deep breaths with eyes closed. The music is classical. The postludes consist of:

1. individual reporting (without interference from other group members);
2. a comparison of the individual's imagery to real life situations and feelings conducted by the therapist with participation from group members;
3. group discussion.

For each of these three activities the therapist chooses, in advance, a specific goal and focuses on it during the postlude.

A music and art activity, adaptable for any population, "Trio" aids clients in the identification and expression of their current emotional state. Each person is provided with three sheets of paper and drawing utensils. They listen to three pieces of classical music, drawing on one sheet during each piece. At the conclusion of the third piece they are instructed to title each drawing. In the postlude each client displays and describes his pictures, comparing the three to each other, and identifying any relationships. The session concludes after a group discussion in which group members comment upon each other's artwork. A trio of pieces I found particularly effective for provoking emotional contrasts was the slow movement of Beethoven's *Emperor Concerto*; followed by "Mars" from Holst's *The Planets*; concluding with the waltz movement from Berlioz' *Symphonie Fantastique*.

In "Short Story," each group member writes a story suggested by a single piece of music. In the induction the therapist suggests a local or simple situation with an eye towards a preconceived session goal. As in "Trio," the postlude begins with each individual reading their story, noting the relationships between the story and real life situations, and ends with a group discussion.

"Movement," analogous to the previous two activities, uses body movement where the others have used drawing and writing. Because some adults are particularly sensitive about public display of their bodies in motion, I have found that the use of scarves can take the pressure off people to "perform," and that they will use movement freely in their sporting with brightly colored silk scarves when they would otherwise feel too intimidated. During the postlude group members describe their impression of their own movements and that of the group as a whole.

Music and Imagery for Relaxation

GIM is not for relaxation. GIM works toward goals. In instances where relaxation in itself is the goal GIM may be applied, but there is a drawback to so doing; i.e., GIM evokes movement in imagery through its use of classical music. Unlike nearly all other forms of music, which are basically static in their presentation of musical material, classical music evolves continuously. In an altered state of consciousness the continuous development of musical material in classical music pushes the psyche forward, creating psychological and physical tensions which are perfect for goal oriented therapy, but are counterproductive to the sedative goal of relaxation. There are some pieces of classical music in which the composer eschews the more typical evolutionary structures and chooses instead simpler structures such as are common in other genres. A noted example is the very popular Pachelbel *Canon* in which an eight measure harmonic structure is repeated over and over. Baroque music contains many examples of pieces in which structural complexity is passed over in favor of a more hypnotic presentation of two alternating ideas. Historically, the concept of development in music is linked to the beginning of the Classical period, although it can be found earlier; and certainly not all Baroque pieces are suitable for relaxation. However, the vast majority of good Baroque music is of inestimable value in music aided relaxation.

The therapist using music and imagery for the goal of relaxation may wish to use the basic structure of the GIM session by altering the emphasis of the components. The prelude consists of a thorough explanation of the procedure as its specific goal: relaxation. The relaxation component of the session is expanded considerably and is used to relax the body. In the induction component the therapist helps the clients to free their minds from all thoughts by concentrating on a relaxing image suggested by the therapist. No guiding occurs (whether for group or individual) in the music/imagery synergy portion. The music is used to sustain the feeling of relaxation created by the previous two components. The piece played in the music/imagery synergy component of the session may be used in the future by the therapist or by the client himself as a method of swiftly attaining a state of relaxation. Unlike GIM in which the postlude can be long and involved, and in which the therapist brings the client back to the state he was in prior to the GIM session, the postlude of a relaxation activity is short and, significantly, the therapist directs the client to maintain a level (though reduced) of relaxation reached.

McCorkle and Clark (1981), in a study on music therapy assisted childbirth considered the mother's preference before constructing music relaxation tapes for labor and delivery. In Hanser's review, "Music and Stress Reduction Research," she reports that Stratton and Zalanowski found a significant correlation between the degree of relaxation and liking for the music.[1] (I myself find it quite difficult to relax during a dental appointment if the dentist has his radio tuned to a popular music station. Nevertheless, when I'm being drilled I want to know that my dentist is relaxed in his job, so I will often forgo my own preference.) Relaxing music (in the music therapy literature referred to as sedative music) has not been clearly defined, though there have been numerous attempts. Munro (1984), in *Music Therapy in Palliative/Hospice Care*, reports that relaxation tapes consisting of the patient's favorite pieces,

---

[1]Suzanne Hanser's review "Music therapy and stress reduction research" is an excellent summary of this subject.

easy listening popular music, or environmental sounds have been helpful in reducing stress in palliative care. "New age" music is also used in inducing a relaxed state of consciousness.

In a relaxation session with alcoholics I discussed the positive features of relaxation, and the negative effects of tension upon the mind and body, in the prelude. I explained that I would be doing a "tense/relax exercise," and that I would then give them something to think about during the music to help them relax. "When the music is over—it will last seven minutes—we'll share briefly about how you felt."

After the clients had found a comfortable place on the floor upon which to lie I employed Jacobsen's progressive relaxation technique followed by a deep breathing exercise; and then, in the induction, instructed, "Allow yourself to clear your mind of all your thoughts. Allow them to fade further and further away, allow your mind to become more and more clear, more and more open. You may begin to imagine for yourself a room. This is a room that you have never been inside before—an imaginary room, that you can create for yourself now. You will create it step by step from the floor to ceiling to furniture, and it can be just the way you'd like it to be. Your room will be a place where you can really relax and be comfortable. This is a place just for you. Let's begin with the carpet. Allow the carpet to become a relaxing, comfortable color. Now the walls. Now the ceiling. Give yourself a comfortable place in the room to lie down. You can lie down and look around you. Begin to fill in the room with chairs, if you wish; or curtains, if there are windows; pictures; anything you'd like. Everything you put in the room will help you to relax.... And your finishing touch will be a stereo system. From the stereo will come very relaxing music which will allow your body and mind to be totally present in your room now, totally involved in your feeling of relaxation, and totally enjoying your experience. As the music comes on the stereo, bring it into your room, put a 'Do Not Disturb' sign on the door, lock your door, and for the next seven minutes you can just relax."

When the music, the second movement from Mozart's *Symphony No. 34*, was finished I said, "Allow yourself to keep your eyes closed and to experience your feeling of relaxation. In your imagination look around your room one last time. This is a place you can go back to whenever you wish to relax deeply. It is a place where no one else may enter. Now, take your 'Do Not Disturb' sign down, and begin your return to our room here. Remember that you can always return to your imaginary room, so you can leave it behind now, but bring with you your feeling of relaxation. Stretch out each part of your body—toes, legs, arms, hands, torso, neck; really stretch. As you are ready, open your eyes and sit up." The group members reported their experiences, briefly describing the visual aspects of their room, and their feelings of relaxation (or lack thereof).

TEN

THE USE OF GIM WITH VARIOUS POPULATIONS

*She said: "What is the most beautiful thing you have
ever seen?"*
*He replied without hesitation: "The sinking of
Atlantis."*
*"It was about three years ago. And God! It was lovely!
It was all ivory towers and golden minarets and silver
balconies. There were bridges of opal, and crimson
pennants and a milk-white river flowing between lemon-
colored banks. There were jade steeples, and trees as
old as the world tickling the bellies of clouds, and
ships in the great sea-harbor of Xanadu, as delicately
constructed as musical instruments, all swaying with
the tides. The twelve princes of the realm held court
in the dozen-pillared Coliseum of the Zodiac, to listen
to a Greek tenor sax play at sunset.*

*"The Greek, of course, was a patient of mine—
paranoic. The etiology of the thing is rather
complicated, but that's what I wandered into inside his
mind.... He's playing again and you've doubtless heard
his sounds, if you like such sounds at all. He's good.
I still see him periodically, but he is no longer the
last descendant of the greatest minstrel of Atlantis.
He's just a fine, late twentieth-century sax-man.*

*"Sometimes though, as I look back on the apocalypse...
I experience a fleeting sense of lost beauty—because,
for a single moment, his abnormally intense feelings
were my feelings, and he felt that his dream was the
most beautiful thing in the world."*

He refilled their glasses.
            —from *THE DREAM MASTER* by Zelazny[1]

Because GIM is such an exciting therapeutic technique it is very tempting to the therapist to use it in any situation in which music listening is part of the treatment process. Nevertheless, GIM is useful only with those populations in which the client (1) is capable of symbolic thinking, (2) can differentiate between symbolic thinking and reality, (3) can relate his experience to the therapist, and (4) can achieve positive growth as a result of the GIM therapy.

---

[1]*The Dream Master* is a work of science fiction.

In GIM the client penetrates beyond literal reality into the depths of the psyche. The deeper he progresses, the more symbolic is the imagery. In Fawn's session (see Chapter 6), the symbolic representation of her mother is an octopus. A person who lacks the ability to think abstractly (as in many cases of mental retardation, organic mental disorder, and neurological impairments) is restricted to literal thinking. To them, an octopus is always an octopus, and their mother is always their mother. They are unable to think metaphorically and therefore can have no imagery in which their mother, for example, could be represented symbolically.

Whereas using GIM with people incapable of abstract thinking is futile, though benign, the use of GIM with people unable to distinguish fantasy from reality is dangerous. In persons showing the psychotic symptom of hallucinations (sensory experiences which do not exist outside the mind) or the psychotic symptom of delusions (false, persistent beliefs resistant to reality testing) not only can an imagined octopus be representative of a mother, but it is also quite literally, an octopus. Hallucinations and delusions are symptomatic of various adult and childhood psychotic disorders (including schizophrenia), organic mental disorders (including senile dementia), and paranoid disorders. Due to the lack of reality referents in GIM the GIM experience is easily assimilated into psychotic fantasies, thereby reinforcing them. A therapist's first priority in dealing with this type of client is to dispel the psychotic fantasies. Other techniques using music are well suited for this approach. Music making activities are valuable because the client directs his energy into the real world. Music listening in which familiar music or music with lyrics is used is also healthy when the client's attention is directed to the way in which the subject matter reflects reality.

The verbalization of the imagery experience during (in the case of the individual sessions) or after (in the case of the group sessions) the music/imagery synergy is an essential element of the GIM technique. Persons with inadequate verbal ability to communicate their experiences are unsuitable for GIM. An unnerving emotional experience in GIM can become traumatic when left to fester unexpressed. The verbal limitations of autistic children and those people who suffer from severe speech defects rules out these groups as potential clients for GIM, as well as many patients rehabilitating from traumas such as head injury or stroke. In the case of the rehabilitating patient who cannot communicate verbally, the re-establishment of their ability to communicate with the outside world is a priority, and GIM which requires extensive verbal interchange between client and therapist could be premature.

Though the imagery evoked in a GIM session has aesthetic qualities that may amuse and intrigue the therapist, the validity of GIM as a therapeutic technique rests on its capacity for giving insights for the solution of problems in the real world. Fawn's symbolization of her mother in the form of an octopus is an exciting image, but it is of no earthly use to Fawn unless she can act upon it. Thus, it is not until Fawn recognizes that she needs to "stomp on the tentacles" of the octopus and finds an appropriate way to do just that, that GIM proves itself relevant to her therapy. Whether or not the client has the ego strength necessary for the accomplishment of real world activity elicited by GIM may not be evident until after the treatment is underway. Insufficient ego strength, as in the case of Nancy (see Chapter 7) indicates that GIM is not valuable as treatment. No harm comes from this, as no harm comes from having a dream and then forgetting it, but simply dreaming is not a time-effective means of treatment for the client who cannot take the steps necessary for action. (It may often take several sessions before it can be recognized that GIM, though harmless, should not be the treatment of choice.)

The more intensive GIM therapy is, the more ego strength it takes to integrate imagery into real life. Individual sessions, because they are deeper, require more ego strength than group sessions. In group sessions with more restricted goals GIM can be beneficial to the clients, whereas individual sessions with the same clients on a short-term basis may be ineffective. Individual sessions with persons with affective disorders such as major depression, bipolar (manic-depressive), manic, dysthymic, and cyclothymic disorders are most effective in long-term treatment.

One final contraindication for the use of GIM is the application of the technique with those clients who, during the period of treatment, are abusing drugs or alcohol. Alcoholics and drug addicts must be abstinent prior to the beginning of therapy. In addition, hospitalized patients other than those with substance use disorders are likely to be taking some type of medication as part of their treatment. This affects their response in GIM therapy, but the extent to which it does has not been studied. Peach, as mentioned previously, suggests that anti-depressant medication may stimulate imagery in depressed persons, concluding that they "may benefit most from imagery therapy" (Peach 1984, 33). Whereas antidepressant medication may indeed stimulate imagery, the presence of imagery is not a meaningful standard for determining the validity of the usage of GIM.

GIM is a significant therapeutic tool for the treatment of a wide range of institutionalized people.

When discussing the use of GIM in institutions one is not likely to think of penal institutions, yet Paul Nolan has done some unique work in just this setting. Using GIM to stimulate imagery for diagnostic purposes (as opposed to therapeutic purposes) he had prisoners (incarcerated at the Philadelphia County Prison) rate their imagery and then correlated their rating with the Beck Depression Inventory (Nolan 1982). Nolan also reported excellent results with a short-term forensic client, R., who was diagnosed as having a mixed personality disorder with hysterical and passive dependent features. R. was incarcerated on a criminal charge of aggravated assault on the woman with whom he lived following her attempt to dissolve their eleven-month relationship. He had been imprisoned previously for thirty days after he assaulted his previous girlfriend of three years when she ended their relationship. He had attempted suicide once and had been hospitalized twice previously in psychiatric settings.

R. was able to work through initial dependency issues, experience his "aloneness," and then free himself from the repressed trauma of his grandmother's death through six individual insight-oriented GIM sessions and three weeks of supportive group music therapy. R. showed increased use of support by treatment staff, more activity on the ward assisting patients in reading and writing, and increased understanding of his previously destructive attempts to achieve intimacy with women (Nolan 1983).

Goldberg utilizes the GIM technique in group and individual music therapy with acute hospitalized patients in a short-term psychiatric intensive care unit. She has found four factors to be important for careful selection of these candidates for GIM: the patient's ability during the session to (1) deflect frightening images, (2) ward off overwhelming anxiety, (3) respond to directives when necessary, and (4) maintain reality testing. Through her experience with acute hospitalized patients Goldberg concludes that GIM is particularly effective in addressing problems relating to specific situations, such as divorce (Goldberg 1987).

In *Facilitating Guided Imagery and Music Sessions*, Helen Bonny reported on the use of GIM with clients suffering from a personality disorder. Following a series of twenty 2–3 hour GIM sessions with two clients with borderline personality disorders, she noted that although, "their sessions were characterized by swift changes in mood state, intense abreaction, and some disorientation and confusion,…one is making adequate adjustment outside the hospital, and the second is experiencing optimal adjustment." She warned that caution should be exercised in cases involving personality disorder. Of clients with an obsessive compulsive personality disorder, Bonny states, "the obsessive compulsive can become involved in GIM imagery and experience a gradual loosening of structure supports, more freedom in action and greater expression of warmth in human relationships" (Bonny 1978a, 44–45). All the clients discussed in her first monograph underwent long-term treatment.

In "Music Therapy: A Legal High," Bonny and Tansill (1977, 129) found GIM to be a "positive motivational factor to continue therapy for many reluctant clients" who are substance abusers. GIM can help the client in achieving the first step of sobriety; i.e., Alcoholics Anonymous Step One, Letting Go. GIM clearly elucidates issues which impede progress in therapy and in sobriety, and changes the basic addictive formula from "tension—alcohol—tension reduction" to "tension—GIM—tension reduction" (Summer 1984). GIM allows the exploration of an altered state of consciousness in a healthy manner, dubbed "a legal high" by one of Bonny's clients (Bonny and Tansill 1977, 129).

Persons with affective disorders can be treated very effectively in group GIM sessions, but, as mentioned previously, these clients often do not have enough ego strength to benefit from short-term individual GIM sessions. Institutionalized patients with neurotic disorders such as anxiety, somatoform and psychosexual disorders should benefit from GIM, however no studies with these groups have been reported in the literature at this date. Dissociative disorders have not been treated with GIM and it is probably inappropriate to do so.

Emotionally disturbed children and adolescents (including abused children, and children with disorders of infancy, childhood or adolescence such as conduct disorders, anxiety disorders, eating disorders, those with developmental delays, and adjustment disorders) are excellent candidates for GIM. Normal children, as well, can benefit from the healthy influence of a musically induced altered state of consciousness. I worked with a group of children, 8–11 years old, with GIM at a Head Start program; using GIM as a means of introducing them to creative problem solving and classical music. At Settlement Music School in Philadelphia I adapted group GIM techniques for use with disadvantaged and normal children, ages 4–8. Regarding the latter I had particular success when using simple inductions such as the "Animal" induction previously described in Chapter 6. Also with the latter group I used a GIM-related activity in which the children listened to a markedly shortened version of Wagner's *Ring of the Nibelungen*, afterward drawing pictures of their imagery (Summer 1986).

Mental conditions (those affecting the organ of the brain) are in large part untreatable by GIM. Due to their lack of abstract thinking, most mentally retarded clients cannot be treated therapeutically with GIM. (However, some clients with mild cases of mental retardation may exhibit enough abstract thinking and verbalization abilities to be GIM candidates.) On the other hand, those clients with specific learning disabilities would probably benefit from GIM, though studies are lacking.

In the only published report ("Music and Imagery as Psychotherapy with a Brain Damaged Patient") on GIM with brain damaged clients, Fran Goldberg reports on her work with a woman hospitalized for diffuse brain damage. Hospitalized specifically for unmanageable explosive outbursts, she required supervision for daily living activities. Uncontrollably frustrated and angry, the client's GIM sessions led to the revelation of her generalized distrust and fear of the hospital staff due to the recent death of her father in a hospital. Fearful of her own death, she worked through her unresolved feelings for her father and faced the loss of control over her body and her life. According to Goldberg the commencement of imagery sessions required "concrete stimuli." The client's images were, for the most part, restricted to memories of actual events.

There is much published work discussing the use of music and imagery with medical conditions such as terminal illness, chronic illness and chronic pain. Most of these studies concentrate on the goal of pain relief or relief from the actual illness by using imagery to directly affect pain, tension, or disease progress. As opposed to GIM this type of therapy has a direct goal of pain relief, and is similar in its approach to that of music and imagery-aided relaxation.

In a recent study, Mark Ryder used music-mediated imagery in a directive manner for pain relief with chronic disease/pain patients. The music was improvised by the client group led by the therapist to "reflect and guide, i.e., entrain, the clients' natural images toward mental healing states." He also reported a case study of M. in which negative and frightening images and feelings emerged which interrupted her willingness to participate in health imagery sessions. For cases such as M.'s, Ryder suggested either verbal catharsis within the group session in order to "stay with the unpleasant imagery" or GIM as a "nonintrusive technique for accessing emotional material" (Ryder 1987, 113, 117).

Sara Jane Stokes, in a short-term pilot project with chronic pain patients (who had undergone multiple surgeries, implants, used pain killing drugs, or who were considered disabled), treated nine such patients in five individual and eight group therapy sessions. The third individual session alone was a GIM session used for "emotional support and psychotherapy to evoke suppressed feelings and unconscious material" (Stokes 1985, 19).

Group GIM with the institutionalized elderly client is effective especially in increasing self awareness and self acceptance, and in fostering interpersonal relationship between group members (Summer 1981a).

Helen Bonny has recently developed a series of programmed music tapes to be used with intensive care patients. On two intensive coronary care units, this GIM-related therapy has been found to aid patients by decreasing heart rate, increasing tolerance to pain and suffering, lessening anxiety and depression and affecting positive changes in target behaviors. Both hospitals involved have continued to use the Music Rx tapes as a permanent treatment choice (Bonny 1983).

Music and imagery assisted relaxation has a great potential for use during labor and delivery. During pregnancy GIM aids in helping the pregnant mother deal with pain or discomfort, changes in her body, fears of childbirth, emotional issues surrounding the birth of a child, and also brings to the fore positive aspects of the self for self nurturance and balance. Though untested, GIM during pregnancy would most probably alleviate post partum depression and facilitate the transition from expectancy to motherhood (Summer 1985b).

Little or no work in GIM has been done with the physically disabled, hearing impaired, visually impaired, or those with speech disorders, orthopedic or neurological impairments. Studies would be welcome.

ELEVEN

CONCLUSION

> *Mind, n. A mysterious form of matter secreted by the brain. Its chief activity consists in the endeavor to ascertain it own nature, the futility of the attempt being due to the fact that it has nothing but itself to know itself with. From the Latin "Mens," a fact unknown to that honest shoeseller, who, observing that his learned competitor over the way had displayed the motto "Mens conscia recti," emblazoned his own shop with the words "Men's, women's and children's conscia recti."*
>
> —from *The Devil's Dictionary* by Ambrose Bierce

We are what we imagine. All of our experiences are subjective interpretations of our mind. Because we "know" that the mind is enclosed in our skull it is most often considered "within" us. Thus, our inner world imagines that we are part of an outer world and interprets all of the objective information relayed to us by our contact in the outer world, our senses. The residence of our awareness, the brain, is a paradox. The brain functions because of chemical changes which promulgate what we think of as thought. Yet what causes these chemical changes? Our thoughts? (To move your left arm, you must first think the command, "move my left arm"; a command which must be preceded by the thought, "think the command that commands 'move my left arm'"; an infinitely inward spiral of antecedent thoughts.) The absurdity of the paradox has prompted the mystics and philosophers of all cultures to conclude repeatedly and independently that thought transcends the physical processes of the body. The implications of this include the concept of the soul, and the reasonable idea: I am God.

The scholars of the Vedanta concluded Athman = Brahman, which means that the individual conscious self equals the omnipresent, omniscient and eternal self. Not only am I God, but in fact, we are God. Thus the idea of plurality, of individuals, is banished on the transcendent level that (with some self-proclaimed possible exceptions) none of us single units of the universal consciousness ever attain. Humanistic therapy is an attempt to move ever closer to the impossible achievement of universality. Unlike other therapeutic stopgaps it does not isolate and treat symptoms, symptoms of our lack of total perfection. Whereas a therapist of another cloth might banish an unacceptable behavior with a reward of food or the punishment of discomfort, a humanistic therapist looks inward, to the universal consciousness, and attempts to enlighten the individual who has strayed from the path of inner awareness.

Guided Imagery and Music, a tool for the humanistic music therapist, is no treatment of symptoms; rather it is an exploration of the inner world by the "client" and a guide, in search of that path towards inner awareness.

Humanistic therapists, when peering into the inner world, see a melange of interconnected positive aspects and past experiences. There are inherent potentials for maintaining homeostasis and for movement in all human beings. Our self-maintenance processes include self renewal, healing and adaptation. To "reach out beyond ourselves to create new structures and new patterns of behavior" (Capra 1983, 285) we contain self transformation processes, which include learning, evolution and development. Humanistic therapy views the human organism as a system, embedded in larger systems (for instance, society and family) whose components are all interconnected and interdependent. Illness results from patterns of interconnected disorders that become manifest at various levels of the organism, and in various interactions between the organism and the larger systems in which it is embedded. Mental illness, Capra defines, is a "multidimensional phenomena involving the entire spectrum of consciousness" (Capra 1983, 322). It can enter the system we define as "I" in various ways. Therefore, restricting approaches to treatment of mental illness restricts our ability to cure it.

Mental illness and physical illness are but two aspects of the existential dilemma of the human condition. Ultimately, the only way to transcend the individual problems of individual existence is to experience one's existence in a broader, cosmic context. The dualism of the subjective (internal) versus objective (external), of the self versus other, of life versus death, is the core of the philosophy of humanistic therapy.

Humanistic therapy is primarily an orientation towards the whole of psychology rather than a distinctive area or school of thought. It requires a multi-levelled approach to therapy to describe different facets of the psyche. The theories of Freud, Jung, Reich, Rogers, Skinner and Laing are all necessary to the humanistic therapist. Ruud quotes the Articles of Association of the American Association of Humanistic Psychology as defining the role of humanistic psychology as, "Concerned with topics having little place in existing theories and systems: e.g., love, creativity, self growth of the organism, basic need gratification, self-actualization, high values, being, becoming, spontaneity, play, humor, affection, naturalness,warmth, ego-transcendence, objectivity, autonomy, responsibility, meaning, fair play, transcendental experience, peak experience, courage and related concepts" (Ruud 1980, 43–44). This definition exemplifies the radical approach to human psychology of the humanistic music therapist. Illness is not the focus; wellness is.

BIBLIOGRAPHY

Achterberg, J. (1985). *Imagery in healing: Shamanism and modern medicine.* Boston, MA: New Science Library.

Arieti, S. (1967). *The intrapsychic self.* New York: Basic Books.

Bonny, H. L. (1975). Music and consciousness. *Journal of Music Therapy, 12*(3), 121–135.

Bonny, H. L. (1977). *Music and psychotherapy.* Unpublished doctoral dissertation, Union Graduate School.

Bonny, H. L. (1978a). *Facilitating Guided Imagery and Music sessions: GIM Monograph #1.* Baltimore, MD: ICM Books.

Bonny, H. L. (1978b). *The role of taped music programs in the GIM process: GIM monograph #2.* Baltimore, MD: ICM Books.

Bonny, H. L. (1980). *GIM therapy: Past, present and future implications: GIM monograph #3.* Baltimore, MD: ICM Books.

Bonny, H. L. (1983). Music listening for intensive coronary care units: A pilot project. *Music Therapy, 3*(1), 4–16.

Bonny, H. L. (1985). *Music: The language of immediacy.* Paper presented at the National Coalition of Arts Therapies Association National Conference.

Bonny, H. L., & Pahnke, W. N. (1972). The use of music in psychedelic (LSD) psychotherapy. *Journal of Music Therapy, 9*(2), 64–87.

Bonny, H. L., & Savary, L. M. (1973). *Music and your mind.* New York: Harper and Row.

Bonny, H. L., & Tansill, R. B. (1977). Music therapy: A legal high. In G. F. Waldorf (Ed.), *Counseling therapies and the addictive client.* Baltimore, MD: University of Maryland.

Bruscia, K. (1987). *Improvisational models of music therapy.* Springfield, IL: Charles C. Thomas.

Bush, C. (1988). Dreams, mandalas and music imagery: Therapeutic uses in a case study. *Arts in Psychotherapy, 15*(3), 219–226.

Capra, F. (1983). *The turning point.* New York: Bantam Books.

Clark, M. E., & McCorkle, R. R. (1981). Music therapy assisted labor and delivery. *Journal of Music Therapy, 18*(2), 88–100.

Copland, A. (1952). *Music and imagination.* New York: Mentor.

DiLeo, F. (1975–1976). The use of psychedelics in psychotherapy. *Journal of Altered States of Consciousness, 2*(4), 325–338.

Ehrenzweig, A. (1953). *The psychoanalysis of artistic vision and hearing.* New York: Julina Press.

Fine, L. J. (1979). Psychodrama. In R. J. Corsini (Ed.), *Current psychotherapies.* Itasca, IL: F. E. Peacock Publishing Co.

Gaston, E. T., & Eagle, C. T., Jr. (1970). The function of music in LSD therapy for alcoholic patients. *Journal of Music Therapy, 7*(1), 3–19.

Goldberg, F. S. (1987). *Guided imagery and music as group and individual treatment for hospitalized psychiatric patients.* Unpublished paper.

Goldberg, F. S. (1989). Music psychotherapy in acute psychiatric inpatient and private practice settings. *Music Therapy Perspectives, 6,* 40–43.

Goldberg, F. S., Hass, T. M., & Chesna, T. (1988). Music and imagery as psychotherapy with a brain damaged patient: A case study. *Music Therapy Perspectives, 5,* 41–45.

Grof, S. (1976). *Realms of the human unconscious: Observations from LSD research.* New York: E. P. Dutton and Co.

Hanser, S. (1985). Music therapy and stress reduction research. *Journal of Music Therapy, 22*(4), 193–206.

Horowitz, M. (1970). *Image formation and cognition.* New York: Appleton-Century Crofts, Inc.

Kenny, C. (1985). Music: A whole systems approach. *Music Therapy, 5*(1), 3–11.

Kovach, A. (1975). Shamanism and GIM: A comparison. *Journal of Music Therapy, 22*(3), 154–65

Kretschmer, W. (1965). Meditative techniques in psychotherapy. In R. Assagioli (Ed.), *Psychosynthesis: A collection of basic writings.* New York: Penguin Books.

Leuner, H. (1965). Initiated symbol projection (W. Swartley, Trans.). In R. Assagioli (Ed.), *Psychosynthesis: A collection of basic writings.* New York: Penguin Books.

Leuner, H. (1969). Guided affective imagery: A method of intensive psychotherapy. *American Journal of Psychotherapy, 50*(1), 4–22.

Lindauer, M. S. (1969). Imagery and sensory modality. *Perceptual Motor Skills, 29,* 203–210.

Maslow, A. H. (1971). *The farther reaches of human nature.* New York: The Viking Press.

Munro, S. (1984). *Music therapy in palliative/hospice care.* Saint Louis, MO: MMB Music, Inc.

Nolan, P. (1982). *The use of guided imagery and music in the clinical assessment of depression.* Unpublished masters thesis, Hahnemann University.

Nolan, P. (1983). Insight therapy: GIM in a forensic psychiatric setting. *Music Therapy, 3*(1), 43–51.

Pahnke, W. N., et al. (1970). The experimental use of psychedelic (LSD) therapy. *JAMA, 212*(11), 1856–1863.

Peach, S.C. (1984). Some implications for the clinical use of music facilitated imagery. *Journal of Music Therapy, 21*(1), 27–34.

Perls, F. (1974). *Gestalt theory verbatim.* New York: Bantam Books.

Quittner, A. L. (1980). *The facilitative effects of music on visual imagery: A multiple measures approach.* Unpublished masters thesis, Florida State University.

Rider, M. (1985). Entrainment mechanisms are involved in pain reduction, muscle relaxation and music-mediated imagery. *Journal of Music Therapy, 22*(4), 183–192.

Rider, M. (1987). Treating chronic disease and pain with music-mediated imagery. *Arts in Psychotherapy, 14*(2), 113–120.

Ruud, E. (1980). *Music therapy and its relationship to current treatment theories.* Saint Louis, MO: MMB Music, Inc.

Sarbin, T. R. (1972). Imagining as muted role-taking: A historical linguistic analysis. In P. Sheehan (Ed.), *The function and nature of imagery.* New York: Academic Press.

Sarbin, T. R., & Juhasz, S. (1970). Toward a theory of imagination. *Journal of Personality, 38,* 52–76.

Sheehan, P. (1967). A shortened form of Betts' questionnaire upon mental imagery. *Journal of Clinical Psychology, 23,* 386–387.

Stokes, S. J. (1985). *A holistic approach to chronic pain.* Unpublished paper.

Summer, L. (1981a). Guided imagery and music with the elderly. *Music Therapy, 1,* 39–43.

Summer, L. (1981b). Tuning up in the classroom with music and relaxation. *Journal of the Society for Accelerative Learning and Teaching, 6*(1), 46–50.

Summer, L. (1983). *The use of music as a catalyst for involvement in imagery.* Unpublished masters thesis, Hahnemann University.

Summer, L. (1984). *The use of guided imagery and music with alcoholics.* Unpublished paper.

Summer, L. (1985a). Imagery and music. *Journal of Mental Imagery, 9*(4), 83–90.

Summer, L. (1985b). *The use of music in the birth process.* Paper presented at the American Association for Music Therapy Conference.

Summer, L. (1986). *Introducing children to opera through improvisation and imagery.* Paper presented at the Association for Music and Imagery Annual Conference.

Summer, L., & Roby, N. (1981). *Reaching the addictive personality through imagery, art and music.* Paper presented at the Delaware Valley American Art Therapy Association Conference.

Tame, D. (1984). *The secret power of music.* Rochester, VT: Destiny Books.

Wylie, M. E., & Blom, R. C. (1986). Guided imagery and music with hospice patients. *Music Therapy Perspectives, 3,* 25–28.